CLASSIC *f*M
LIFELINES

M GUSTAV
AHLER

AN ESSENTIAL GUIDE
TO HIS LIFE AND WORKS

JULIAN HAYLOCK

PAVILION

First published in Great Britain in 1996 by
PAVILION BOOKS LIMITED
26 Upper Ground, London SE1 9PD

Copyright © Pavilion Books Ltd 1996
Front cover illustration © The Hulton Deutsch Collection 1996

Edited and designed by Castle House Press, Llantrisant, South Wales
Cover designed by Bet Ayer

A CIP catalogue record for this book is available
from the British Library

ISBN 1 85793 982 4

Set in Lydian and Caslon
Printed and bound in Great Britain by Mackays of Chatham

2 4 6 8 10 9 7 5 3 1

This book can be ordered direct from the publisher.
Please contact the Marketing Department.
But try your bookshop first.

Contents

ACKNOWLEDGMENTS

To Mum, Dad, and my sister Clair,
for all their love and kindness,
and for always being there
when it counted most

With grateful thanks to Eileen Townsend Jones of Castle House Press, whose boundless expertise and enthusiasm were a constant source of inspiration throughout the writing of this book.

A NOTE FROM THE EDITORS

A biography of this type inevitably contains numerous references to pieces of music. The paragraphs are also peppered with 'quotation marks', since much of the tale is told through reported speech.

Because of this, and to make things more accessible for the reader as well as easier on the eye, we decided to simplify the method of typesetting the names of musical works. Conventionally this is determined by the nature of the individual work, following a set of rules whereby some pieces appear in italics, some in italics and quotation marks, others in plain roman type and others still in roman and quotation marks.

In this book, the names of all musical works are simply set in italics. Songs and arias appear in italics and quotation marks.

CHAPTER 1

SCENES FROM CHILDHOOD
(1860–75)

- *Humble beginnings*
- *Move to Jihlava*
- *Early training*
- *First concerts*

Gustav Mahler's relatively short life spanned one of the most crucial periods in the history of classical music. Behind him lay the rich Romantic pastures of Bruckner and Brahms, and ahead the otherworldly musical landscapes of Schoenberg, Berg and Webern. It is a sign of his seminal importance and all-embracing vision that he earned the respect and admiration of all of these composers.

The last great inheritor of the Austro-German symphonic tradition, Mahler expanded the scale of music to near-bursting point – there are single movements in his works that last longer than an entire symphony by Mozart or Haydn. He also stretched the accepted system of major and minor keys to its limits, taking music to the very brink of keylessness (atonality). He confessed in later life to the composer Sibelius that each of his symphonies embraced a 'whole world' – his literary tastes, neuroses, responses to 'nature', and most particularly in Mahler's case, the inexorable cycle of life and death. His influence has extended far into the present century, whether it is directly felt – as in the music of Shostakovich and Britten, in particular – or acts as a divine example for the likes of Boulez and Stockhausen.

Perhaps the single most extraordinary fact about this amazingly popular figure is that he was effectively a part-time composer. Indeed, most of his life was devoted to his career as one of the world's most sought-after conductors. His pioneering methods of concert preparation and opera production were to set the standard for the rest of the century, exerting a profound influence on conductors as apparently disparate in approach as Herbert von Karajan and Leonard Bernstein. Many feel that the constant tension between the creative and recreative side of Mahler's genius was in part responsible for hastening his early demise.

Mahler's life was a series of seeming contradictions, intimately bound up with his complex background. Although nominally of Bohemian extraction, Mahler was born into the ailing Empire of Franz Joseph I, and was therefore technically classed as a native Austrian. He also constantly fought against the unavoidable religious and political implications of his own Jewishness. Although essentially proud of his ascendancy, he attempted to calm the turbulent waves of anti-Semitism by becoming a Roman Catholic in 1896, and then marrying a Gentile in 1901. His profound sense of unease is made tangible in the slow movement of his *First Symphony*, where a Jewish-styled episode is lampooned in the context of a funeral march. This lack of firm roots had an emotionally destabilizing effect on Mahler. Towards the end of his life, despite having by then won international acclaim, he despondently reflected:

> *I am condemned to homelessness thrice over, as a Bohemian among Austrians, as an Austrian among Germans, and as a Jew throughout the world.*

Mahler was born on 7 July 1860 in the Bohemian village of Kalischt. His parents were Moravian Jews of very little means, and the nearest major centre, Jihlava (Iglau), was more than forty kilometres away. During an outing in 1896 with his close friend and confidante Natalie Bauer-Lachner, Mahler gave an account of his humble beginnings. As they wandered past a row of dilapidated peasant hovels, he reflected:

> *I was born in a place just like that; there weren't even any window panes. There was a pond in front of the house. The only dwellings for miles around were a few isolated huts.*

Mahler's stern and inflexible father, Bernhard, had gradually hauled himself up the social ladder from the level of a lowly carter to operating a ramshackle distillery on a small plot of land in Kalischt. His mother Marie, 'a soap-boiler's daughter' according to Mahler, was of a more gentle disposition and was forced into the loveless marriage against her will. She bore Bernhard fourteen children in all, and despite suffering since birth from a limp and a heart condition, was made to work like a slave. Bernhard was an abuser who thrashed the children according to his mood, and regularly beat his wife. On one particular occasion, she sustained such appalling injuries that the memory of the event was burned on Mahler's memory. During a session with the pioneering psychoanalyst Sigmund Freud, shortly before Mahler's death, he remembered running screaming from the house to the strains of a hurdy-gurdy playing outside. Small wonder that, given such an appalling family background and such uneasy religious and political roots, Mahler matured into a highly insecure, neurotic adult.

Mahler developed feelings akin to hatred towards his father, but was utterly devoted to his mother. Indeed, he deified her extraordinary resilience in the face of such adversity. As a result, he found relationships with women difficult in later life, partly because of the man-and-wife 'relationship' he had witnessed as a child, and partly because any woman with whom he came into contact was invariably compared to his 'saint-like' mother. Nevertheless, Mahler's unstinting admiration for her was tinged in his young mind by a profound lack of respect for any creature who could allow such horrors to be regularly bestowed upon herself and her children. It is somewhat ironic that the physical scars left by his father amounted to no more than a good bruising, whereas those left by his mother were to plague him to the end of his days. He suffered both from a psychosomatic nervous tic in his right leg, which made his movements slightly ungainly, and he inherited his mother's heart defect, the deciding factor in his relatively early death.

Death itself was to play a major part in Mahler's early life – far beyond the norm, even in an age when child mortality was an everyday occurrence. Gradually, one by one, he lost virtually all his brothers and sisters. Five succumbed to diphtheria in early childhood, and his beloved brother Ernst died in 1874 of the inherited heart disorder. Leopoldine succumbed to a brain tumour in 1889 (the year both their parents died), while another brother, Otto, shot himself in 1895. Two brothers and two sisters survived into the twentieth century, although it was only the latter, and in particular Justine, who were to play any kind of role in Mahler's day-to-day life. Indeed, both sisters became so entwined in their genius brother's world that they ended up marrying distinguished musician friends of his, the brothers Eduard and Arnold Rosé.

The Mahler family's move to Jihlava shortly after Gustav's birth was facilitated by a decree from Franz Joseph that offered increased freedom of movement for Jews within the Empire. This turned out to be something of a mixed blessing, as Jihlava's population was dominated by Germans with decidedly anti-Semitic leanings. The new house was a comparatively humble dwelling, from where Bernhard ran his distillery business. Yet it produced one unexpected bonus. One day, the four-year-old Gustav went missing, causing the family grave concern. Having spent most of the day combing the streets of Jihlava, they eventually found him up in the attic, apparently oblivious to the panic he was causing, tinkling away on an antiquated piano. Mahler's ability to lose himself in a kind of dream world was utterly characteristic of his early years. Although the dreadful things that went on around him hurt him deeply, he instinctively protected himself by a form of denial, preferring instead to create alternative worlds from within when those without were so painful. This was also a particularly effective weapon against his father. His instincts as a composer were already being shaped.

For young Gustav, the move to Jihlava proved to be utterly crucial, as the town boasted a thriving musical community. This was centred around the Musical Society, which arranged seasonal programmes of orchestral concerts based on a staple diet of Mozart and Haydn. We can assume that the standard of the orchestra must have been at least passable, as roughly half of its thirty-four members were paid professionals. Productions at the local opera house included Mozart's *Don Giovanni* and Bellini's *Norma*, and oratorios by Mozart and Handel were frequently performed by the town's choral society. In addition, there was a fine town band, founded and conducted by Jihlava's musical 'father', Heinrich Fischer. The band was to have a profound influence on Mahler's own music, both in terms of its sonorities (trumpet calls in particular), and his predilection for march rhythms in general. Fischer was to become a formative influence, as he lived only a few doors away from the Mahler residence, and, recognizing the boy's talent, gave him his first formal lessons in harmony and counterpoint.

Mahler's musical sensitivities were by no means limited to the concert hall or marching bands. He also taught himself to play the accordion and would delight his family by playing innumerable folk tunes, which he had picked up during visits to the surrounding countryside. Once again, the impact on his mature music is unmistakable. It would seem that his love of popular culture developed out of a passion to set himself against his father, who despite his limited means, harboured pretensions of grandeur and education.

Mahler was not the most attentive or co-operative of pupils, yet his talent was such that by the age of ten he was ready to make his public debut in the autumn of 1870. The event was recorded in the local newspaper, *Der Vermittler*:

> *On 13 October, a subscription concert was given that was quite out of the ordinary. The nine[sic]-year-old son of a local Jewish businessman named Maler [sic] gave his first public performance in front of a packed audience. The fact that he played so well is very much to this future virtuoso's great credit; if only such exquisite playing could have been rewarded with a better-quality instrument. When Herr Viktorin [Mahler's ex-teacher] hears of his extraordinary success, he will certainly feel proud of his former protégé.*

As a result of this public acclaim, Bernhard began to wonder whether the local school at Jihlava was really up to the job of training such an extraordinary talent. Gustav's constant daydreaming and inability to concentrate his attention on his general studies had already resulted in somewhat mediocre reports from the local 'gymnasium' (or high school). Bernhard's solution was to send his son to a gymnasium in Prague for the 1871–72 academic year, under the watchful eye of one Heinrich Grünewald. In the event, Mahler lasted only five months.

The experience appears to have been nothing short of a disaster, according to Alma Mahler, the composer's future wife:

> He [Mahler] was brought down to earth with a bump when he
> encountered the seedier side of life at Grünewald's lodgings in
> Prague, where he had been sent by his father. His clothes and shoes
> were taken from him and worn by others . . . ; he told me he took
> the whole thing in his stride, almost 'took it for granted'. However,
> on one occasion, when sat in a darkened room, he found himself
> the unwilling witness of a particularly violent sexual encounter on
> the part of Grünewald's son, Alfred, and the family's maidservant.
> Mahler attempted to intervene, but was viciously turned upon by
> them both, and then sworn to secrecy.

Bernhard, on hearing about his son's predicament, made straight
for Prague, removed him from Grünewald's house, and brought
him back to the gymnasium at Jihlava. According to Mahler's
memory of the occasion, his father was blazing mad with him for
having caused such a nuisance, but had for once at least done the
right thing by the child.

The next firm evidence we have about young Gustav's musical progress is found in a report in Jihlava's *Mahrischer Grenzbote*,
dated 24 April 1873. This describes a performance given by the
budding thirteen-year-old virtuoso that further underlines his
prodigious technical prowess at this time:

> . . . There followed a performance of Sigmund Thalberg's [fero-
> ciously difficult] Fantasia on Themes from the opera Norma
> for piano, given by the young virtuoso, Mahler, whom we have
> rightly shown much appreciation for in the past. He was every
> bit as breathtaking as his previous performances would have led
> us to expect, and his stunning rendition was rewarded with a
> standing ovation.

Such a glorious reception must have given the ultra-sensitive
Mahler's confidence a substantial boost, and for a while, even life
at home was untypically stable. However, almost exactly a year
later, his thirteen-year-old brother Ernst died from heart failure
after many months of illness. Mahler had stayed with him throughout this period, reading him stories and doing everything in his
power to ease his pain. When the end came, he was utterly
inconsolable.

Following her husband's death, Alma Mahler unearthed an

extraordinarily poignant letter to his friend Joseph Steiner, who was the librettist of his early opera *Ernst von Schwaben* (now lost):

> *Now we are walking along well-trodden paths, and there's a skinny organ-grinder, his hat held out to passers-by. He sings out of tune, but I can still just about make out Ernst von Schwaben's 'Greeting' as Ernst comes towards me with his arms outstretched, and then I realise that it is in fact my dear brother. . . .*

By this time, Mahler's education was doing little more than ticking over, and his musical talent was stagnating in the provincial atmosphere of Jihlava. Fortunately, he was discovered by a travelling musical dignitary, who persuaded Bernhard to take young Gustav to visit Julius Epstein, a professor at the Vienna Conservatory – the *Gesellschaft der Musikfreunde*. Interestingly it was not Gustav's piano-playing that so impressed Epstein, but a small portfolio of compositions he had brought with him, later destroyed. The professor was quite taken aback by the fifteen-year-old's creative talent and immediately arranged for him to be enrolled at the Conservatory. It was therefore during the autumn term of 1875 that Gustav Mahler took his first serious steps towards becoming a seminal figure of twentieth-century music.

Chapter 2
STUDENT YEARS
(1875–80)

- ♦ *Vienna Conservatory*
- ♦ *Befriends Hugo Wolf*
- ♦ *First encounters with Wagner and Bruckner*
- ♦ *Das klagende Lied*

Vienna was not only the nerve centre of the Austrian Empire, but also its greatest musical city. Brahms and Bruckner were its most prominent figures at the time, and composers of the calibre of Tchaikovsky and Dvořák were frequent visitors. Unlike the German-dominated Jihlava, the greater part of the Viennese population consisted of immigrants, whose ease of movement within the empire had been facilitated by the same decree that had allowed the Mahler family to move from Kalischt to Jihlava in the first place.

The magnificent new Vienna Conservatory had been completed as recently as 1870, following a costly expansion on the express orders of the Emperor himself. What had started out as little more than a collection of ill-maintained classrooms, could now boast a number of modern lecture halls, proper practice facilities, and a magnificent new concert hall. This remains the home of the Vienna Philharmonic today, and the place where they still give their annual New Year's Day Concert.

The exact chronology and detail of Mahler's three years at the conservatory between 1875–78 are swathed in obscurity (save for the official records), although much in general terms can be gathered from his reminiscences and those of others during his time there. There is, perhaps, more than a grain of truth in Mahler's somewhat flippant account of his general education in a letter of December 1896, which studiously avoids even mention of the Conservatory:

> *. . . Spent my early years at the gymnasium – learned nothing, but spent most of my time from about the age of four composing, before I even knew what a scale was. When I was seventeen I entered the University of Vienna, but enjoyed more regular attendance at the Vienna Woods than the lecture theatre.*

Although Mahler was financially disadvantaged during his time at the Conservatory, he was no worse off than many of his contemporaries. On the other hand, his life became musically enriched far beyond anything he could have dreamt of in the provincial surroundings of Jihlava. He arrived brimming with talent although short on academic training. In certain respects the Conservatory helped fill the gaps. His knowledge of harmony increased enormously under the watchful eye of composer Robert Fuchs, and he could hardly have wished for a more sympathetic piano teacher than Joseph Epstein, the man who had helped him gain entry to the Conservatory in the first place. Epstein took a fatherly interest in the young virtuoso, treating him more as a member of his own family than a mere student. He even engaged Mahler to give his own son, Robert, piano lessons, thereby ensuring that at least some meagre funds would be guaranteed. His other studies, particularly in counterpoint and composition under Franz Krenn, were largely ineffective – so much so that the director excused Mahler's attendance, from his second year onwards, leaving him to make up any lost ground in later life.

Mahler became socially more adept during his time at the Conservatory, fully indulging in the Bohemian lifestyle common among the young intellectual classes of the day. He became especially friendly with two extremely gifted co-students, the great songwriter Hugo Wolf, and Hans Rott, Anton Bruckner's favourite pupil. Sadly, both relationships were to end in tragedy. Mahler appears to have been drawn to Wolf by mutual genius and poverty. They were instinctively outsiders, and shared lodgings for a while, although Wolf appears to have been more in awe of Mahler's abilities than vice versa. Yet Wolf was already showing signs of the instability that would eventually lead to his total nervous collapse. His behaviour was irascible and he made himself no friends by constantly railing against those in authority. In 1877, he was dismissed for a 'severe breach of discipline.' By the end of his life, his admiration for Mahler had dissolved into spiteful resentment at the latter's success. His final descent into madness was marked by a claim that he had now been appointed Opera Director and that his first job would be to sack Mahler – the then Director. Following a bungled attempt at drowning himself in the Traunsee, he spent the remainder of his days incarcerated in a Viennese lunatic asylum, where he died on 22 February 1903.

Mahler's relationship with Hans Rott was more stable: they enjoyed a far deeper understanding of each other. Yet Rott was also a man with a delicate mental disposition. In 1879, Brahms responded to some music Rott had sent him with the advice that he was totally devoid of talent and should give up. Rott lost the balance of his mind and died a few months later. Brahms, who was both anti-Conservatory and anti-Bruckner, also doled out some fairly severe criticism to both Wolf and Mahler at this time.

It is small wonder that Mahler became so obsessed with death and mortality in his later years, when life all around him must have appeared so fragile. Unbelievably, another close acquaintance, Anton Kripser, also went insane. At least there was one happy outcome from the students enrolled at this time, for the eleven-year-old Arnold Rosenbaum (later Rosé) was destined to become Mahler's brother-in-law.

The most musically informative and influential events in Mahler's student life were to a large extent extra-curricular. Concerts by the Hellmesberger String Quartet (led by the Conservatory principal Joseph Hellmesberger) regularly featured the near-unfathomable late quartets of Beethoven, whose claustrophobic intensity affected the budding composer deeply. Also of crucial importance during his first term was his first exposure to the music of Wagner, via a production of *Tannhäuser*. Wagner himself was present, and the impact of the occasion was further enhanced by Wolf's total veneration of the 'master' at this time.

Mahler's talent for the piano – nominally his first study – and for composition dominated his work at the Conservatory in his first year. In June 1876, he was unanimously awarded prizes in both disciplines by an independent panel – for Schubert's late *A minor Sonata* and the first movement of Mahler's freshly-composed '*Quintet*' respectively. The latter, like so many of Mahler's student compositions, has never come to light, which has led some commentators to assume that the Conservatory made a mistake and that the entry refers in fact to the surviving first movement of a *Piano Quartet*. This prophetic A minor movement was certainly composed at around this time, and is therefore our first and only reliable indicator of the sixteen-year-old Mahler's creative prowess. No one hearing this richly upholstered work could possibly guess its provenance – the arch-Romantic, 'sighing' phrases and autumnal nostalgia are straight out of the Schumann/Brahms copybook. Yet for a mere 'student work' it is unusually accomplished, displaying a penchant for soulfully expressive melody, and a sensitivity for atmosphere that extends to a commendably restrained ending.

Throughout the year, Mahler maintained contact with Jihlava, and through a private tutor continued his general studies in preparation for his finals at his old gymnasium in 1877. During his first summer vacation he gave a concert there, both as pianist and composer. This, according to the original poster, featured the *Piano Quartet* movement and a *Violin Sonata* (now lost), both pieces being described by a local critic as showing 'an exuberance of invention . . . the works of a genius.' Mahler also played a Chopin ballade and Schubert's technically highly exacting '*Wanderer*' *Fantasy*, which was particularly applauded for its 'entirely original interpretation.'

Mahler's second year at the conservatory almost didn't happen, as, embarrassed by severe lack of funds, he rather hastily submitted his resignation. Once again it was Julius Epstein who came to the rescue and secured for him a guarantee from the governors to pay half of his fees for the next term, as well as the director's permission to continue his studies there. Although Mahler did not enter the composition competition that year, he was rewarded with another piano first prize, this time for Schumann's Op.20 *Humoreske*.

The seventeen-year-old Mahler started his final year late, having successfully completed his matriculation back in Jihlava. Perhaps the most important event of this winter term was Mahler's close contact with Anton Bruckner, who at fifty-three years of age was only just beginning to make a name for himself as a composer. Mahler attended a few of his lectures, beginning the start of a close friendship. He was, however, decidedly prickly regarding the subject of his purely academic relationship with Bruckner. In later life, he claimed that he had never actually been his pupil. Whatever the truth of the situation, there is no doubting the sheer impact of his music. Mahler was present at the disastrous premiere of Bruckner's *Third Symphony*, and was one of a group of only twenty or so who were left at the end applauding when the rest of the audience had long gone. He immediately set about making a piano duet transcription of the work.

Although Mahler was now officially listed as specializing in composition, his piano playing was still a strong feature of life at the conservatory. Indeed, the only conclusive evidence we have of a concerto appearance by Mahler occurred during a programme of 20 October 1877, when he played the wrist-cripplingly demanding first movement of Scharwenka's *First Piano Concerto*, written only the previous year. However, at the end-of-year competition, it was as a composer that Mahler won joint first prize, with a *Piano Quintet* movement (now lost). He left the conservatory with his matriculation certificate, and as an added bonus, a diploma, which was awarded only to the most outstanding students.

Mahler spent the following two years furthering his education at Vienna University, teaching the piano in order to raise much-needed funds – and contemplating his future. This was in many respects uncertain, especially as his lowly background made breaking into the higher echelons of Viennese society (let alone asserting his presence as a serious composer) decidedly tough going. He was by all accounts rather highly strung, and according to the reminiscences of his friend Emma Adler, he would often be seen strolling the streets of Vienna gesticulating and talking to himself so demonstrably that messenger boys would come up to him convinced that he had been requesting their services.

Teaching took up more of Mahler's time than he would ideally have liked, but at least it kept him above the bread line. Invariably forthright in his opinions, he remained very sensitive to criticism, and at this stage lacked faith not so much in his own ability, but in others' ability to appreciate it. Indeed, so uncertain was he of pursuing his musical calling, that at one point he seriously considered becoming a poet instead. It is hardly surprising, therefore, that the three major undertakings of this early period – the operas *Rübezahl* and *Die Argonauten* (both now lost) and the cantata, *Das klagende Lied* – were all extensive settings of his own specially written texts.

Mention of *Rübezahl* – the name of a sprite from German folklore, and well known to children – returns us to Mahler's volatile relationship with Hugo Wolf, as recounted in reminiscences by Mahler's future wife, Alma. She tells of how inseparable they were in their early days, and how they had shared money – everything, in fact. Together with another friend, Rudolf Krzyzanowski, they discovered Wagner's *Götterdämmerung* for the first time, and in their enthusiasm bellowed out the great trio between Gunther, Brunnhilde and Hagen 'so horribly that the landlady, beside herself with rage, hurled open the door and told them to vacate the premises immediately. She remained there until all three had gathered together what few possessions they had, and saw them off the premises personally, hurling abuse at them the whole time.'

It was almost inevitable that two such exceptional talents attempting to make a name for themselves in the same place at the same time would come to blows, although their drifting apart was over what appears to have been a relatively minor affair. Once again, according to Alma Mahler:

> *During one particular conversation, Wolf came up with the idea of composing a fairy-tale opera. This was before Humperdinck or anyone else had even thought of such a thing. Of the several subjects they came up with, they settled on* Rübezahl. *Mahler's youthful impetuosity and enthusiasm typically ran away with him to the extent that he sat down that very night and sketched the whole thing out. The next day he set off excitedly to show Wolf the merit of his efforts only to discover that he* too *had been working out a few ideas and was piqued to discover that Mahler had done the same. Taking umbrage, he dropped the whole idea, and although they remained on talking terms, relations between them began to cool off markedly from this point.*

There is typically little reliable documentation with which to place Mahler's activities and whereabouts during the latter half of 1879 with any kind of certainty, although his creative energies must surely have been totally absorbed with *Das klagende Lied*

('The Song of Sorrow'), to which he put the finishing touches the following year. He later revised the score in 1892–93, omitting the first part, making one or two minor changes to the orchestration, and removing the offstage orchestras. The latter were reinstated in the final revision of 1898–99. Nowadays, the work's few recordings and still fewer performances almost invariably revert back to the work's original tripartite structure.

Das klagende Lied shows a marked improvement on the *Piano Quartet* movement. Indeed, it is hard to believe that Mahler could have made such astonishing progress in just four years. The text has a distinctly 'folklorish' flavour, to some extent influenced by the writings of the brothers Grimm. The story tells of two brothers who seek a particular flower in order to win the hand of a beautiful princess. One murders the other, whose body then metamorphoses into a bone flute, which, when discovered by a wandering minstrel, tells its chilling story. The princess gets to hear it just in time to prevent her marrying a murderer.

Mahler's points of stylistic reference have moved forward in time to Wagner and Bruckner, even if the fairy-tale world of man and his place in nature can be operatically dated back at least as far as his beloved Weber's *Der Freischütz* of 1821. What is particularly striking, however, is the clear emergence of such identifiably Mahlerian characteristics as the telling use of an off-stage town band, the ironic juxtaposition of the revelatory and the ordinary, and the range of musical styles he mixes and matches under the same musical roof. Perhaps most notable is the sheer exuberance of the writing, which only very occasionally glories in the full might of the assembled forces, but rather delights in drawing upon various combinations of unusual sonorities.

During the spring of 1880, Mahler composed his first three song settings to have survived intact: '*Im Lenz*' ('Spring'), '*Winterlied*' ('Winter Song'), and '*Maitanz im Grünen*' ('May dance on the green'), all to his own words. The first two are little more than engaging pleasantries derived from the music to *Das klagende Lied*. However, '*Maitanz im Grünen*' (later incorporated in the first set of *Lieder und Gesänge* as '*Hans und Grethe*') is notable for a melodic idea that was later adapted for the second movement of his *First Symphony*. In addition, it betrays the influence of the Austrian *Ländler*, a waltz-like peasant dance in triple time, which was to become the vehicle for some of Mahler's most startling invention.

This year had been a turning point for Mahler. He had not only completed his first major work, throughout which signs of the mature composer intermittently bubble to the surface, but he unexpectedly found himself invited to take up his first professional post – not as a pianist, nor even a lecturer, but as a conductor. Not in his wildest imaginings could Mahler have possibly foreseen that, by the turn of the century, he would have become Europe's most powerful music director.

CHAPTER 3
CONDUCTOR OR COMPOSER?
(1880–91)

♦ First conducting job
♦ Early songs
♦ Lieder eines fahrenden Gesellen
♦ Symphony No. 1

The conducting post Mahler had been offered was at Bad Hall, a spa (or 'Bad') town situated in Upper Austria. He was initially less than keen on the idea, but on the advice of his mentor Joseph Epstein he decided to accept, if only because it sounded more palatable than piano teaching. He was also reasonably confident that *Das klagende Lied* would quickly establish his reputation as a composer and thereby relieve him from any further conducting. Although he moaned a great deal about his lot during his time at Hall, there can be little doubt that this extension of his musical personality became as important to him as composing itself. The two were complementary, for he viewed interpretation as just another form of creativity. Just as surely as composing was the unravelling of the complex workings of his own personality, so the interpretation of other composers' masterworks gave him an insight into their creative psyche that he would otherwise never have enjoyed.

The appointment at Hall involved directing various theatrical and light operetta productions at the local summer theatre. Considering the seriousness with which Mahler approached life, and the style of music to which he was instinctively drawn, these decidedly lowbrow pieces were hardly inspirational. Nor did his responsibilities end there. We learn from Alma that:

His duties included putting out the musicians' parts before each performance, dusting down the piano, and then collecting every-thing back in after the concert. During the interval, he was expected to wheel the theatre director's baby around in her pram. When he was also requested to appear on stage and 'fill in' any missing parts as necessary, he really felt enough was enough. He later looked back on this as something of a missed opportunity, however, for there was much that he could have learnt if only his pride had let him.

Whatever his experiences at Hall were really like, the conducting bug had bitten. Mahler asked if he might also be employed during the winter season, but as there was little work at that time of year, he opted instead to return to Vienna in order to complete *Das klagende Lied*. Although he was overjoyed at the way it had initially turned out, proudly informing friends it was his 'Opus 1', not everything was good news. Even during the short time he had been away, his personal standing with the desperately insular Viennese had cooled somewhat. In addition, he discovered to his great consternation that his friend Hans Rott had gone com-pletely insane following the extraordinary rebuttal by Brahms.

Things hardly improved when, in the summer of 1881, *Das klagende Lied* was rejected outright for the Beethoven Prize – Brahms and Goldmark had led the jury. It went instead to Robert Fuchs, one of Mahler's teachers at the Conservatory, for his *Piano Concerto in B flat minor*. The panel were extremely conservative in outlook, and had clearly put technical expertise before originality. Goldmark felt uncomfortable with this stance and let it be known to the committee that he wanted clearer guidelines to allow sheer talent to be taken more firmly into consideration in future.

That summer, Mahler also secured a second conducting appointment at the Provincial Theatre in Laibach (now called Ljubljana). Here the musicians were distinctly more professional in their attitude, with playing standards to match. Mahler was given a whole range of opportunities, including making his con-cert conducting debut with Beethoven's '*Egmont*' *Overture* in September 1881. One critic neatly summed up Mahler's devel-oping approach to his art when he described it as having been played 'with precision'.

Mahler made his operatic debut with Verdi's *Il Trovatore* on

3 October 1881, which, according to the local paper, 'went without any significant mishap', and followed it up with a full season including Rossini's *The Barber of Seville*, Weber's *Der Frei-schütz*, and Mozart's *The Magic Flute*. The latter drew a particularly enthusiastic response from the *Laibacher Zeitung*, which remarked that the orchestra had been 'meticulously rehearsed with great enthusiasm by Herr Mahler'. *The Barber of Seville* was even relayed over the town's new telephone system to test it for sound quality. Although there was little that could be done with an orchestra of only eighteen full-time players, he raised the playing standards to a level previously undreamt of. Given the almost 'happy-go-lucky' attitude towards operatic performances in the provinces, this was in itself no small achievement.

In addition to conducting, Mahler's services as a pianist were also called upon for a concert with the local Philharmonic Society on 5 March 1882, when he played Mendelssohn's *Capriccio brillant* – accompanied merely by a string quartet – and solo pieces by Chopin and Schumann. Once again it was the brilliance and polish of his technique that were noted with enthusiasm. We learn from Laibach's orchestral leader (and later conductor), Hans Gerstner, that: '. . . [Mahler] was a vegetarian, and regularly joined us at the Rose Inn after each performance, downing a couple of glasses of Pilsner beer.'

Towards the end of the season, Mahler was awarded a benefit concert in recognition of all the efforts he had made during his time in Laibach. This featured Flotow's all-but-forgotten opera, *Alessandro Stradella*, and was greeted with a tumultuous reception, followed by an after-production celebration during which he was presented with a large, ribboned laurel wreath.

The season over, Mahler returned to Vienna for the remainder of 1882, still without a full-time post. As would increasingly become the pattern of his life, he devoted most of his 'spare' time to composition, particularly work on his opera, *Rübezahl* – the first act was completed shortly before Christmas. In addition he appears to have begun serious work on settings of poems by Leander (*'Frühlingsmorgen'* and *'Erinnerung'*) and de Milina (*'Serenade'* and *'Phantasie aus Don Juan'*), which, together with *'Hans und Grethe'*, became his first volume of *Lieder und Gesänge*. Of particular note is *'Erinnerung'* ('Recollection'), which is the earliest published example of a piece by Mahler to begin and end in a different key – a method technically known as 'progressive tonality'. Perhaps the most famous example of this procedure is his *Fourth Symphony in G*, which concludes with a radiant song-setting cast in *E* major.

Mahler briefly returned to his home town of Jihlava during September, where he conducted a performance of Suppé's *Boccaccio*, which once again won special enthusiasm for its technical aplomb. It was also around this time that he reaquainted himself with the talented violinist/violist Natalie Bauer-Lechner, with whom he had fraternized during his years at the Conservatory. She was a most attractive and appealing young lady, and their friendship blossomed over the years, particularly during the 1890s, until Mahler's marriage to another woman. Her devotion to him was such that she recorded in invaluable detail their innumerable encounters.

One of the biggest headaches for any Mahler scholar is trying to tie the composer down to any particular residence for any period of time. Indeed, the details of his early years have proved surprisingly elusive for someone who lived little more than a hundred years ago. His nomadic existence is underlined in a letter to his friend Anton Krisper, in which he claims to have moved into a different district of Vienna every fortnight. In addition, over a period of just three months he had had five separate addresses, not allowing for various hotels he had briefly stayed in. This is a curious symptom of Mahler's wanderlust, presumably as a result of his feeling uncomfortable with the idea of settling down or 'belonging' anywhere in particular.

Just as it looked as though his conducting seasons had been nothing more than a flash in the pan, the twenty-two-year-old Mahler received an urgent telegram early in January 1883, requesting he take over as opera conductor at the Municipal Theatre in Olmütz (now Olomouc), in Moravia. This followed the sacking of the resident conductor, one Emil Kaiser, after a long series of minor disputes with the powers that be and the musicians in his charge.

Olmütz was nothing if not a challenge. Although the theatre there could boast an orchestra and chorus on a scale larger than anything Mahler had so far encountered, the whole operation was under-financed and in a serious state of disrepair. In many ways Mahler, with his authoritarian high standards, was just what the company needed, even if it took some musicians and critics a little while to be convinced of the fact.

One of the most complete pictures of Mahler's standing at any stage in his early career is painted by the then principal baritone at Olmütz, Jacques Manheit, who recounted Mahler's impact on the company some twenty-five years later, in 1908. Mahler's first production was Meyerbeer's *Les Huguenots*. Having put the fear of God into just about everyone in the company, and worked the singers until they were literally hoarse, he put the whole thing together in just three days.

The first performance was not without its problems:

At the end of the first act, the singer who was playing Marcel stormed backstage towards his dressing room, in a terrible state of excitement: 'I can't possibly sing for this man. One minute he is holding his baton in his right hand, the next it is in his left, and all the time his free hand keeps crossing his face so that I can't see when I'm supposed to come in.' When Mahler heard about the problem he calmly explained that 'conducting makes me overheat and brings me out in a sweat so that my pince-nez keep falling off the end of my nose and I have to use my spare hand to catch them on the way down.'

Apparently, when Mahler re-emerged for the second act he had tied his glasses on with a pair of red ribbons, which caused such hilarity that the company were extremely lucky to make it to the end in one piece. Mahler's eccentric behaviour extended to the inn afterwards where, in among the rolling crowds full of wine and beer, he proceeded to ask for a large helping of spinach and a bowl of apples. Then it was on to the coffee house next door, where progress was constantly hampered during a game of billiards as Mahler insisted, much to the clientele's general hilarity, on intermittently conducting the whole of Act I of *Les Huguenots* with his cue.

Hardly surprisingly, there were few in the opera company who wanted to have anything to do with the intense young man 'out of hours' – which in any case suited the budding composer down to the ground – yet in time they came to respect the complete integrity, not to say effectiveness, of his methods. A letter written to Mahler's friend Friedrich Löhr, just the day before Wagner's death on 13 February, presents his side of the story no less vividly:

> *From the time I first arrived in this place, I felt that the judgment of God was upon me. . . . Thank God I have so far managed to keep Mozart and Wagner out of it as it would be inconceivable to even attempt such as* Don Giovanni *or* Lohengrin *with such a motley crew. . . . I try desperately to heighten their levels of musical awareness, yet my most fervently passionate entreaties are more often than not met with looks of meek sympathy or sheer disbelief.*

Mahler chose for his benefit concert Méhul's *Joseph*, which he described as 'an uncommonly likeable work'. With less than a full strength of singers, and without a producer or stage manager, he somehow pulled the whole thing together – even his most vociferous detractors sat up and took notice. By the time he departed from Olmütz, even the word 'genius' was heard occasionally being whispered along the corridors of power.

His return to Vienna at the end of the season was comparatively short-lived, as Mahler promptly found himself offered yet another conducting post, a temporary contract as Royal Assistant Conductor and Chorus Master, to oversee a series of Italian opera productions in Kassel. This had come about as the result of a recommendation from a Karl Überhorst, who had been bowled over by Mahler's production of Flotow's opera *Martha*, during his time at Olmütz.

In the May of 1883, Mahler left Vienna to take up his second new appointment of the year. Having satisfied everyone as to his competence, he signed a three-year contract, to run from the following October. The Kassel theatre was run like a military operation by one Baron Adolf Gilsa, and Mahler was left in no doubt as to his wide-ranging responsibilities by the comprehensive list he was given. These included training the chorus, making any necessary alterations to scores to make them more playable, orchestrating songs and short pieces for the company to sing and play, and even composing short works that the theatre might deem necessary for ceremonial or gala occasions.

Kassel was Mahler's first serious appointment as a conductor, although in many ways the opportunities it presented were more in theory than in practice. This was largely the result of the jealous behaviour of the principal conductor, Wilhelm Treiber, who, naturally enough, creamed off all the best music for himself, leaving his young assistant to take care of the lighter works and operetta. It was not all one-sided, however, for in the January of 1884, Mahler had a crack at one of his favourite operatic scores, Weber's *Der Freischütz*. The critics were generous in their praise, once again tending to applaud the extraordinarily high technical standards he encouraged, while advising caution regarding certain aspects of his interpretation, particularly his unpredictable tempi. His impulsive physical gestures were also diametrically opposed to the reserved manner of the podium generally favoured at the time.

Mahler's natural impatience to further himself rather backfired on one particular occasion. The great musical pedagogue, conductor and pianist Hans von Bülow visited Kassel to conduct, and so inspired Mahler that he felt compelled to write him a somewhat conciliatory letter, decrying his experiences at the theatre. Bülow tactlessly passed the letter on to Treiber, who was then able to strengthen his own position by bringing it to the theatre manager's attention. No direct action was taken, but the letter was placed in Mahler's files for future reference.

It was also during his spell at Kassel that the highly impressionable Mahler appears to have fallen deeply in love for the first time, according to Alma Mahler with two singers simultaneously, to whom he sent poems of his own composition. Unbeknown to him, they were friends and poked gentle fun at their mutual admirer behind the scenes, comparing letters he had written them. Whatever the truth of this story, he certainly appears to have fallen head over heels in love with a Johanna Richter. Right up to the time of his departure from Kassel in June 1885, he had remained hopeful of some sort of requitement, but it was not to be. It was her rejection of his most sincere advances that directly resulted in the composition of Mahler's first indisputable masterpiece, the *Lieder eines fahrenden Gesellen* ('Songs of a Wayfarer').

This glorious cycle of four settings of Mahler's own text is not only one of his most shamelessly tuneful works, but also forms a repository for many of the ideas subsequently developed in the *First Symphony*. Given its mere fifteen-minute duration, it runs through a remarkably wide range of emotions, hurtling the listener from the rustic, open-air innocence of '*Ging heut' morgens über Feld*' ('Went across the fields this morning'), to the blistering vehemence of '*Ich hab' ein glühend Messer*' ('I have a glowing knife'). Once again, Mahler treats tonality not so much as a unifying device as yet another highly potent weapon in his expressive armoury. None of these songs end in the key in which they set out – as the traveller goes on his journey through life, so we travel musically with him. The songs remained in piano-accompanied form until Mahler finally found time to orchestrate them in the mid-1890s.

Work on the *Gesellen Lieder* was unusually protracted, partly because of his conducting duties, but also due to his having to compose some incidental music to a popular best-seller, Joseph Victor von Scheffel's poem, *Der Trompeter von Säkkingen*. This was turned around in just two days in the form of seven *tableaux vivants*, was critically well received, and enjoyed several performances in centres outside Kassell. Mahler subsequently disowned it as 'rubbish', and destroyed virtually the entire score. However, one movement has survived, as Mahler later incorporated it into the early versions of his *First Symphony* between the first and second movements. Its name? *Blumine*. Originally intended to convey the impression of a trumpet playing a serenade across the moonlit Rhine, the principal theme of this hauntingly beautiful movement is recalled as the 'big tune' in the symphony's finale.

Mahler certainly went out with a bang at Kassel. Despite Treiber's attempts to undermine the whole operation by pulling out and taking the theatre orchestra with him, Mahler organized a festival, inviting the five largest local town choirs to take part. Originally he had hoped to tackle Beethoven's *Ninth* ('*Choral*') *Symphony*, but by default decided that it would be safer to settle on Mendelssohn's less exacting oratorio, *St Paul*. The performance on 29 June seems to have been a rip-roaring success, so that, in spite of Mahler's by now irredeemable relationship with the theatre authorities, the five choral societies and scratch orchestra were thoroughly delighted with the results. Mahler was presented with a diamond ring, a commemorative album, laurel-wreath, and a gold watch. The latter went to the pawnshop the very same day, due to the composer's severe lack of funds.

Mahler's frustration over his untenable position at Kassel and the abortive affair with Johanna had already led him to seek work

elsewhere. During July 1885 he completed a successful proba-
tionary period as assistant conductor at the Leipzig Municipal
Theatre, which led directly to his temporary appointment for the
1886–87 season. This left him with a whole year in-between jobs
– with absolutely no prospect of regular employment. Quite out
of the blue, one of Mahler's orchestral contacts, Angelo Neumann, came to the rescue with the offer of a short-term post as
principal conductor at the Royal German Theatre in Prague.
Neumann had something of an expert's eye for spotting conducting talent. He had already singled out Artur Nikisch, among
others, and one of his later protégés was a certain Otto Klemperer.
He was not alone in feeling that Mahler was rather overactive on the
podium, but was otherwise an electrifying presence, already capable
of handling the big guns of the repertoire.

Accordingly, having tried Mahler out on Cherubini's opera,
Les deux journées, Neumann put him straight in at the deep end
with Mozart's *Don Giovanni*, Wagner's *Die Meistersinger*, and the
company's first-ever productions of the latter composer's *Das
Rheingold* and *Die Walküre* (the first two parts of his *Ring* cycle). This
was Mahler's first serious outing with scores of such a nature, and
the results were generally acclaimed, even if once again his
flouting of tradition caused certain reservations on the part of the
press. Mahler passed comment on the matter in a letter of 6
September 1885 to his mother and family back in Jihlava:

> By 'tradition' they [critics] really mean in the style of time-honoured
> (i.e. unquestioning) productions of the past. I never let them get
> to me, and invariably still go my own way. . . .

As before, Mahler was not merely restricted to conducting opera
during his stay in Prague. He also directed two concerts from
memory, the first of which, on 21 February 1886, featured a performance of Beethoven's *Ninth Symphony*, a work he had been longing
to conduct for years, in addition to an extract from Wagner's
Parsifal, written only four years earlier. The critics were ecstatic:

> He shaped the phrases and melodies of each movement by the
> most intimate gestures of face and hand. . . . Everyone instinc-
> tively felt that Herr Mahler's conducting brought out the very
> best in the work. . . .

Another concert was noted not only for fine interpretations of Mozart's late *Symphony in G minor* and the scherzo from Bruckner's *Third Symphony*, but also three of his own songs for voice and piano, one of which appears to have been '*Hans und Grethe*', which made such an impression that it had to be immediately encored.

Mahler had been so successful in Prague that he regretted having to take up the promised post in Leipzig. Despite attempts to get out of the contract, the authorities there would not release him, so that following a brief visit to his parents in June, he moved on to take up his post at the New State Theatre, artistic home of the then budding young conductor Artur Nikisch. The two, being naturally extremely wary of each other, appear to have been more-or-less at daggers drawn from the start. We learn from a letter of early October that:

> *I have very little to do with him at all; he is very cold and continually keeps his distance – either out of disdain or insecurity – I've really no idea! Basically, we walk past each other without uttering a single word!*

By the end of the month, Mahler had become so fed up with playing Nikisch's lackey that he was already considering looking for a new position. The situation came to a head when, in November, it became apparent that the forthcoming production of *The Ring*, part of which had been originally promised to Mahler, was to be conducted by Nikisch in its entirety. Even the critics had made a political football out of the situation, invariably coming down on the side of the already-established Nikisch. There was certainly no shortage of requests for Mahler's services, for in addition to an invitation to return to Prague, doors were opening in Karlsruhe, Hamburg and New York.

This was all highly unnerving for the twenty-six-year-old Mahler, for the facilities at Leipzig were vastly superior to anything he had experienced before. He formally resigned, but the authorities still would not let him go. At the eleventh hour, fate intervened. At the end of January 1887, having conducted *Das Rheingold*, Nikisch fell extremely ill with a severe lung infection and was forced to retire from the rest of the season. Mahler was thrust into the limelight, having to cope with *Die Walküre* at extremely short notice. The critics were highly enthusiastic, giving special praise to the orchestral preludes that open each of the three acts. The orchestra found his exacting standards too much to bear, however, and made a formal complaint to the authorities. To the latter's eternal credit, they stood by Mahler one hundred per cent. In any case, it seems that the members of the orchestra were in the habit of such behaviour, having doled out exactly the same treatment to Nikisch some years before.

Much of the summer and autumn was devoted to a new project that had come about as the result of contact with the composer Weber's son Carl. The latter had for some time been trying to find a composer who would be willing to take on the task of completing his father's comic opera, *Die drei Pintos*. This had been left in the form of a series of incomplete sketches, often with nothing more than the vocal parts written out. Both Meyerbeer and Lachner had already given up in the attempt. Mahler at first found the undertaking somewhat daunting, but his devotion to the task knew no bounds once he had got fully into his stride. To fill in the missing sections he even went so far as to use less familiar pieces by Weber so as to create as authentic an atmosphere as possible. In all this he bluntly refused to change a single note of Weber's original.

The premiere in January 1888 was attended by music directors from all over Germany, distinguished academics, the famous Viennese critic Eduard Hanslick, and even a representative from the Metropolitan Opera in New York. It scored a resounding success, and Mahler gained special pleasure from the fact that several passages singled out for special praise by the critics as 'authentic' Weber had been almost entirely of his own creation. He received a handsome fee from the publishers – this was his first orchestral score to appear in print – and the work's subsequent performance in several other opera houses (including Vienna) guaranteed a healthy income from royalties. Mahler had become a celebrity almost overnight, his music receiving approbation – if only by the back door – the like of which he had never enjoyed before. Even Richard Strauss praised it, much to the annoyance of his mentor Hans von Bülow, to whom Mahler had written his obsequious letter during his time at Kassel.

It was inevitable that working on the Weber score would have reawakened Mahler's own natural creative facility – indeed, the process had already started. During 1887 he seems to have discovered Achim von Arnim and Clemens Brentano's collection of folk poetry, grouped together under the title *Des knaben Wunderhorn* (a friend of Mahler's later claimed that he had known the book since childhood). Its celebration of nature and its vein of gentle, popularist rusticity and naiveté strongly appealed to Mahler, all of whose subsequent song settings (bar one) until 1901, were drawn from this single volume.

During 1888, Mahler fell hopelessly in love with another woman, this time Carl Weber's wife Marion. It would appear that on this occasion his feelings were to some extent reciprocated, and she even seems to have considered running away with him at one point. It was inevitable that his churning emotions would once again find a natural outlet in music. Mahler set to work on a symphonic poem – composed in all its essentials in just six weeks during March and April – that would eventually crystallize into his *First Symphony*. This is all the more remarkable given that it was for the most part written in the early morning and late evenings, around his regular work at the theatre.

The work we now know as the *First Symphony* was originally in five movements – it was not until 1896 that the *Blumine* movement was finally removed. We learn from a letter to Max Marschalk of 20 March 1896, during Mahler's work on the final revision:

> *The third movement (a funeral march) was in fact based on the well known children's painting,* The Huntsman's Burial. *Yet I didn't seek to portray anything in particular – it was more a question of generating precisely the right mood, after which the fourth movement suddenly bursts forth, like a fork of lightning. . . .*

In another revealing letter to the conductor Franz Schalk, who prepared a celebrated performance of the symphony in March 1898, we learn that Mahler required the fullest possible complement of strings. In addition, he requested that the first movement be played with the greatest delicacy throughout (except, of course, for the big climaxes), and that the finale should erupt with unreserved power and venom, with a strengthened horn section at the end. The third movement was to be played with a touch of macabre humour, and the scherzo's trio very tenderly.

There was also a gentle reminder that the very opening should represent 'the sounds of *nature*, not of music'. The symphony also establishes the *Ländler* style of 'dance-scherzo', which would subsequently find a place in almost all Mahler's symphonies, excepting *Nos.3* and *8*.

The *First Symphony* gives the most poignant expression to the cross-fertilization in Mahler's music between symphony and song. The main theme of the opening movement is derived from the second of the *Lieder eines fahrenden Gesellen*, while the final song of the same cycle furnishes the second trio section of the funeral march. This much-maligned movement, the nerve-centre of the symphony, most graphically nails Mahler's stylistic leanings to the mast. A minor-key version of '*Frère Jacques*' – its first announcement on the lumbering double-bass full of irony – is set against a number of contrasting episodes that variously recall marching town bands and Jewish popular music. These are highlighted by intentionally ludicrous offbeat 'oom-pah' accompaniments, replete with string *pizzicati* (plucking) and *col legno* (using the wood of the bow).

The surrealistic effect of this extraordinary movement is heightened when set against its partners, a subtly scored opening movement that atmospherically evokes the sounds of nature, followed by a swaying *Ländler*. The no-holds-barred Tchaikovskian finale demonstrates an all-conquering spirit that makes this the most emotionally conventional of the four movements, despite a number of digressions to recall previous material en route. Largely uncelebrated in its own time, the *First Symphony* is now one of Mahler's most widely played works.

Mahler's final months at Leipzig were, professionally speaking, less than happy. Having won such acclaim with *Die drei Pintos*, he found returning to the mundanities of being a largish cog in a very large wheel simply too onerous. In any case, his public standing was such that he felt impelled to move on and take charge of his own destiny. Resigning from Leipzig, Mahler made a temporary return to Prague in the summer, during which time he prepared and directed five performances of *Die drei Pintos*, and started preliminary work on a symphonic movement in C minor (the *Todtenfeier*), which would be adapted some five years later as the first movement of his *Second Symphony*.

Mahler had changed a great deal since his last contact with

Prague, and within only a month he had tendered his resignation, citing irreconcilable artistic differences. However, such was by now his reputation that in a matter of just a few weeks he already had another conducting post lined up – as music director of the Royal Opera in Budapest.

CHAPTER 4

FROM BUDAPEST
TO VIENNA
(1891–97)

♦ *Budapest*
♦ *Death of parents*
♦ *Hamburg*
♦ *Second and Third Symphonies*

Whatever Mahler's problems with those in authority and some of the musicians in his charge over the years, he had won the unstinting support of a small but highly influential number of distinguished musicians. Among them was Guido Adler, professor of music at Prague University, who made fervent representations on Mahler's behalf for the post of artistic director and chief conductor of the Royal Hungarian Court Opera. This, combined with Mahler's obvious talent, resulted in the twenty-eight-year-old being signed up with a ten-year contract at the handsome salary of 10,000 florins per annum, starting in September 1888. In the event he stayed only three years, although by the end of his term there, his reputation was secure.

Mahler had something of a tendency to be appointed to establishments that were in serious need of improvement, and Budapest proved to be no exception. Only four years before, the court opera had moved into magnificent new premises, with a fine orchestra, increased funds, and excellent facilities. Yet due to bungling and unadventurous management, it was already stagnating on Mahler's arrival, losing money hand over fist, employing foreign singers it couldn't really afford, and relying on a cripplingly small repertoire that no longer captured the public's imagination.

The new music director typically tackled the problem head-on. Playing upon the prevailing mood of nationalistic fervour that gripped Hungary at this time, Mahler decided that henceforth all productions would be sung in Hungarian, and foreign 'guest' appearances would be reduced to the bare minimum – and only then if the artist spoke Hungarian. In the past, productions had featured native artists singing in Hungarian and guests using their own language, making an absolute nonsense of stage action and credibility. Rather ironically, Mahler spoke next to no Hungarian himself, and had at first to work entirely through an interpreter.

In addition, in order to raise technical standards, Mahler grouped the singers and players together to form a central core, expecting them to rehearse regularly without resorting to deputies. There had already been public outrage at Mahler's huge salary, as well as the fact that he was a virtually unknown non-Hungarian – and a Jew at that. Mahler clearly had his work cut out. The eyes of the Hungarian capital were upon him.

Mahler bided his time, keeping the public waiting for his conducting debut. Behind the scenes he was preparing the company for a *Ring* cycle, tackling every conceivable aspect of production to ensure that standards were uniformly high. Count Albert Aponyi, then a member of the Hungarian Parliament, remarked on Mahler's multifarious activities at this time:

> *Mahler is not just a musician – unlike a number of other conductors I could name – but is equally adept at stage management and directing; this ensures that a production with Mahler at the helm is a complete artistic entity . . . I have never encountered someone with such well-rounded and widely-embracing gifts.*

It was not until January 1889 that Mahler made his long-awaited first appearance at the helm of a new, all-Hungarian production of Wagner's *Das Rheingold*, followed shortly by *Die Walküre*. His success was universal, winning over pro- and anti-Wagnerians alike. Many held these to be the finest Wagner performances ever to have been held outside Bayreuth itself – superbly produced, magnificently sung and played. For his part, Mahler was unhappy at not being able to produce this glorious music in its original language and his own tongue – German. His frustration increased when he was forced to concede that he simply did not have the local talent to do justice to planned productions of *Siegfried* and *Götterdämmerung*. In any case, audiences were getting decidedly unhappy about all the German-language material he was conducting. The local papers were also becoming increasingly unsettled about the fact that, since Mahler had taken over, not a single serious Hungarian opera had been produced. It was therefore decided to brighten up the atmosphere with some ballet and light opera.

As if all this were not enough, things at home were far from happy. At the tail-end of the recent Wagner productions, Mahler was sent word of the death of his father in February. Concern for his mother's material well-being was doubled when he discovered that she *too* was seriously ill, and that his sister Justine, who was looking after her, was close to nervous collapse. He could stand being separated from them no longer, and, dropping everything in Budapest, made directly for Jihlava. From here, he took his sister and mother to Vienna for a badly-needed break and to receive assurances from a doctor that her condition was not life-threatening. However, once more at Jihlava, her health worsened dramatically and she died on 11 October.

Mahler's already heightened emotional state was hardly helped by the news that year that his sister Leopoldine had also died of a brain tumour. He extended an invitation to Justine to move in with him – ostensibly as his housekeeper, although in reality she was not up to the job. Alma Mahler tells us that Justine was so weak that Mahler had to carry her up four flights of stairs to his apartment every day. Meanwhile, his other surviving sister, Emma (then still only fourteen), and brother, Otto, were in the care of Mahler's close friend Friedrich Löhr.

The end of the year climaxed in two performances of works by Mahler himself. The first featured three of his new songs, which received general critical approval both for Mahler's pianism and his music. However, the premiere of the *First Symphony* on 20 November – simply entitled 'Symphonic Poem' at this time – inspired a somewhat mixed reaction. Those close to Mahler were genuinely astounded by the work's striking originality and proliferation of ideas.

A report that appeared in the *Nemzet* newspaper also positively glows with enthusiasm:

> *This symphony is the impassioned work of a youthful, unquench-*
> *able talent, barely containing its seemingly inexhaustible ideas*
> *within a traditional framework . . . wild applause broke out at*
> *the end of every movement.*

That same 'applause' was interpreted rather differently in some quarters – and by Mahler himself – as increasing unrest being voiced by the conservative majority in the audience. The *New Pest Journal* summed it all up when it commented that audiences will 'always be pleased to see him [Mahler] with baton in hand, just as long as he's not conducting one of his own works.'

All in all, the symphony's premiere was a disappointment, and combined with the stress of the demise of his mother and the consequent need to worry about his brothers and sisters Mahler was brought to the verge of a total collapse in the spring of 1890. He could hardly have asked for a more nurturing recu-peration than his first trip to Italy with his sister Justine, followed by a summer holiday in the beautiful Hinterbrühl area just outside Vienna. Here he found time to put the finishing touches to the second and third volumes (totalling nine songs altogether) of his *Lieder und Gesänge*, all derived from the folk-poetry collection *Des knaben Wunderhorn* ('The Youth's magic horn'). These, along-side the twelve-song collection actually entitled *Des knaben Wun-derhorn*, formed another repository from which were derived ideas for the *Second* and *Third Symphonies* in particular. The finale of the *Fourth Symphony* is yet another *Wunderhorn* setting.

The remaining *Lieder und Gesänge* are more mature in outlook than the first volume, hardly surprisingly given the seven-year gap involved. Mahler's distinctive creative voice registers with far greater clarity throughout, his unique stylistic gregariousness miraculously held together under the same creative umbrella. The spirit of military music is recalled in '*Zu Strassburg auf der Schanz*' ('On the battlements at Strassburg') and '*Aus! Aus!*' ('Over! Over!'), so too the *Ländler* style in '*Selbstgefühl*' ('Self-con-fidence'), while Mahler's unmistakable vein of dry humour is given free rein in '*Starke Einbildungskraft*' ('Vivid imagination') and '*Um schlimme Kinder artig zu machen*' ('To make naughty children good'). '*Ablösung im Sommer*' ('Relief in summer') was to inspire the third movement of *Symphony No.3*. We learn from Löhr that Mahler was at his most relaxed and at one with nature for much of the time, although as his thoughts turned to planning the new season back at Budapest, his mood downturned accordingly.

When he eventually returned to Hungary during the September of 1890, Mahler found the general atmosphere decidedly more chilly than it had been six months earlier. Nevertheless, he saw out the year with an epoch-making production of Mozart's *Don Giovanni*, which won the unstinting admiration of even the arch-detractor Brahms, who quite uncharacteristically went so far as to embrace Mahler publicly on stage.

During his absence, those who were still incensed at having a non-national running the state opera house had gradually gained the upper hand – Mahler's head was effectively on the block. Areas of the press clamoured for his resignation, and when a new Intendant was appointed – one Count Géza Zichy – the latter promptly made it known that he had his eye on Mahler's job. Several quarrels ensued, escalating to the point that Mahler even found he had been locked out of his own office. He tendered his resignation on 14 March 1891 – but not before having first secured a contract with the director of the Hamburg State Opera, Bernhard Pollini.

His final production in Budapest was Wagner's *Lohengrin*, where the 'pro' lobby were so vociferous that they brought the first act to a standstill, repeatedly chanting his name. It is unlikely that Mahler enjoyed having the work of the 'master' interrupted in such a manner, although the gesture itself must have meant a great deal to him under the circumstances. For those with eyes to see and ears to listen, Mahler had totally transformed the Budapest opera from a going-nowhere operation to a leading force in the operatic world, attracting visitors from all the major centres. They would never see his like again.

Although in Hamburg Mahler had nowhere near the sort of autonomous control over repertoire and productions that he had enjoyed in Budapest – and the salary was also marginally lower – the playing and singing standards were of a truly international standard. For the first time in his career, there was no need to drag a company up to an acceptable professional level. This was just as well, as there was no settling-in period for Mahler. He was thrown straight in at the deep end with a schedule of conducting an average of eighteen different operas a month, with very little time for any rehearsing in between. These were no lightweight undertakings either. In one week in March alone he conducted both *Siegfried* and *Tannhäuser*, and then, during May, one of the most famous-ever productions of *Tristan und Isolde*.

His impact was immediate. Joseph Sittard in the *Hamburg Correspondent* reported:

> *Herr Mahler is not only in complete control of the notes, but also the spirit of every score he conducts; this is communicated effortlessly both to his fellow musicians and to the audience. Every entry is cued in, every change in dynamic properly observed; Herr Mahler binds the whole performance together with a magnetic energy which is quite spellbinding. This had clearly communicated itself to the orchestra, for there were times when the audience could hardly believe they were listening to the regular theatre orchestra, so marked were the improvements.*

Hans von Bülow, by far and away the most prominent musical force in Hamburg's musical life, was present at one of the performances of *Siegfried* and wrote excitedly to his grown-up daughter Daniela:

> *. . . Hamburg now has a first-class conductor in the form of Gustav Mahler . . . who in my opinion is right up there with the very best. . . . I saw him rehearsing one day and could hardly believe the way he kept that musical rabble exactly where he wanted them. . . .*

It would seem that after the sticky start in Kassel, von Bülow had very much fallen under the spell of his younger rival – at least as far as his conducting was concerned. When von Bülow took a nasty fall, hardly more than a year after Mahler's appointment, he requested the composer stand in as his deputy. Following von Bülow's tragic death in Cairo in February 1894, it was also Mahler who stood in to conduct the remainder of his season, dedicated to his memory. As to Mahler's creative side, von Bülow had always been unconvinced, although in fairness he had little to go on save for some of the early *Wunderhorn* settings and the first movement of the *Second Symphony*, which he found overlong. Indeed, when he first heard Mahler play through the movement to him in private, von Bülow is supposed to have remarked, only half in jest,

'If that is music, then I know less about music than I thought.' During 1892, he had been due to direct a concert featuring some of Mahler's songs, but felt that emotionally he simply could not get inside them. Mahler deputized for him.

Having put his first two months in Hamburg behind him – an amazing total of thirty-five productions – Mahler was too exhausted to even consider serious composition during the summer vacation. Instead, he decided to get away from it all, going on a lengthy tour around Scandinavia, where the breathtaking scenery exerted an almost hypnotic effect on the highly impressionable musician. Meanwhile, the Hamburg Theatre had received a complete refit, including the introduction of electric lighting for the very first time.

Mahler's first full season at Hamburg included several important productions, including Beethoven's *Fidelio*, which one reviewer noted as demonstrating a slightly self-conscious approach. Slow music was apparently drawn out excessively, *pianissimi* were barely audible, and dynamics greatly exaggerated. But, perhaps most gratifying of all, was a production of Tchaikovsky's *Eugene Onegin*, then only two years old and being given its first performance outside Russia. Mahler had done all the legwork, leaving it to Tchaikovsky to conduct the final rehearsal. But things did not go at all well, and when it came to the night Tchaikovsky decided – apparently to the orchestra and singers' total surprise – to let Mahler take the helm, while he sat in the audience. Everything went extremely smoothly – to Tchaikovsky's great satisfaction and profound relief. In addition, Mahler also directed a number of other early performances of important operatic works, including Puccini's *Manon Lescaut*, Verdi's *Falstaff* and Humperdinck's *Hänsel und Gretel*.

The summer break of 1892 was highlighted by a German opera season in London, which Mahler appears to have been offered by default when the great Hans Richter could not be secured. Mahler was in two minds whether to accept, as this would mean the second summer in a row that he would be unable to do any serious composing, but he relented when he realized this would further establish his reputation abroad, and also gave him an opportunity to brush up on his patchy English. The performances took place at Covent Garden and Drury Lane, and although Mahler appears to have found the orchestral standards rather disappointing, he had nothing but praise for the casting, which included many distinguished German singers. The composer of *The Sorcerer's Apprentice*, Paul Dukas, was present at a performance of *Fidelio*, which he later described as 'one of the most incredible musical experiences of my life'.

Mahler returned to Hamburg during the September, having delayed the trip as the city was held in the grip of a cholera epidemic that reached a peak when, on just one day, more than six-hundred-and-eighty new cases were reported. Theatre director Pollini was not in the least sympathetic, as Mahler had thereby broken the terms of their contract, and at one point threatened to fine him more than a year's salary. Eventually the situation cooled down, but the two never returned to their former good relations.

Mahler's extraordinary workload continued unabated as the new season got underway, with one sixteen-day period in January 1893 that featured thirteen performances, with a different opera being performed every night. This punishing schedule included five performances of Mascagni's *L'Amico Fritz*, spread evenly throughout the schedule, alongside such awesome undertakings as *Die Walküre*, *Siegfried*, *Tristan*, *Lohengrin*, *Fidelio* and the *The Magic Flute* in between.

1893 proved to be a red-letter-year for Mahler as it witnessed his return to serious creativity, initially with a long-postponed revision of the *First Symphony*, which, at this stage still remained in five movements, but was now given the subtitle '*Titan*', after the novel by Jean Paul.

Following the end of the season, Mahler discovered a wonderful hideaway overlooking a lake in Steinbach-am-Attersee. So taken was he with the scenery that he decided to have built a small house down near the lake's edge, where he could go to compose. This was installed by the following summer.

Meanwhile, he composed the *Andante* of the *Second Symphony* in just seven days. As Natalie Bauer-Lechner recollected, Mahler was full of enthusiasm for the movement:

> *The only way to compose is to give it your all. It simply doesn't work if you start out with a little motive which you then submit to all manner of extensions and fugal devices until at the end you get a whole movement. I can't stand composers who do this;*

*you should just let the music flow from within and preferably be
left with plenty to spare at the end. . . .*

The scherzo was also composed at this time, alongside several
song settings that Mahler originally called *Humoreskes*, which were
later collected together as part of *Des knaben Wunderhorn*. This
collection was not finally completed until 1898, although its close
relationship with the *Second* and *Third Symphonies* in particular
make it worth considering briefly here in its entirety.

By taking folkloristic poetry and transforming it into something sophisticated enough to satisfy concert hall audiences,
there were many who felt that Mahler had lost something of the
naive innocence of the originals. But for Mahler this was all part
of the assimilation process – he had taken the texts and made
them his own. It was only at the stage that he began to live
through them that they became elevated to an even higher plane
of expression – the symphony. One of the settings, *'Urlicht'*
('Original light'), was to become the fourth movement of the
Second Symphony, and *'Des Antonius von Padua Fischpredigt'* ('St.
Anthony of Padua's sermon to the fish') forms the basis of the
scherzo. *'Das himmlische Leben'* ('Heavenly life') re-emerges as the
finale of the *Fourth*. Other songs can be heard floating subliminally
in and out of the textures.

Throughout, Mahler uses his instrumental forces sparingly,
the odd martialistic blast from the percussion merely employed
as local colour. Indeed, military music raises its head on a number
of occasions, most touchingly in *'Wo die schönen Trompeten blasen'*
('Where the fair trumpets sound') where it becomes integrated
into the *Ländler* style with exquisite subtlety. *'Verlor'ne Müh'*
('Labour lost') and *'Rheinlegendchen'* ('Rhine legend') are even
referred to as *'Ländler'* by Mahler in the manuscript, although for
many it is the livelier settings that resonate in the memory, such
as *'Lob des hohen Verstandes'* ('Praise of lofty judgement'), which is
replete with onomatopoeic 'cuckoos' and 'hee-haws', and *'Trost
im Unglück'* ('Solace in misfortune'), with its delightful exchanges
between hussar and maiden.

On 27 October, Mahler as composer scored his greatest
public success to date when he conducted the first performance
of his newly revised symphonic poem *Titan*, alongside several of
his new songs. The audience roared their approval, and one of the

songs had to be encored, although the critics were typically tepid in their response. Despondent about the latter, Mahler's mood was not helped when he heard, towards the end of the year, that his new songs had been rejected by the famous German music publishers, Schott.

During February 1894, Mahler learned of the death of von Bülow in Cairo. In response he composed the finale of his *Second Symphony*, on which he appears to have begun working on the very day of von Bülow's funeral service in Germany, 29 March 1894. This setting of Klopstock's words, 'Rise up again, yea, that dust shall rise again after its brief repose', was completed during the summer at the little hut at Steinbach.

The *'Resurrection' Symphony*, as it became popularly known, calls for a massive array of forces, including ten horns, eight trumpets, and a large percussion section. From Mahler's correspondence, we gather that the guiding light of the *Second Symphony* was not its thought processes, but its emotional content:

> *Images still drift in and out of my mind when listening to certain passages. . . . The correspondence between 'pure' music and life's experiences may be more intimately linked than anyone had so far been prepared to acknowledge.*

Regarding the *Todtenfeier* ('Funeral Ceremony') first movement – composed back in Prague in the September of 1888 – we learn that it represented the hero of the *First Symphony* being carried to his grave. It was also intended as a reflection of the philosophical question 'What is the meaning of life?' The rest of the symphony finds our hero looking back over his life, first to times of innocence and happiness in the second movement, and then the grip of reality really takes a hold in the Scherzo third:

> *He despairs of himself and God. . . . Utter disgust for every form of existence and evolution seizes him in an iron grip, tormenting him until he utters a cry of despair.*

'Stirring words of simple faith' (Mahler's words) illuminate the *'Urlicht'* fourth movement, raising the curtain on a massive thirty-five-minute finale. This runs the whole gamut of emotion, from the desperate uncertainty of the opening, as the dead emerge from their graves, seeking an answer to the eternal question of life and death, to the transfiguration through love and understanding that forms the central message of Klopstock's hymn. This final passage reaches a fever pitch of emotional intensity, utterly devastating in its impact.

Mahler later withdrew his programmatic indications, citing that the work was quite capable of standing on its own, and that in any case its underlying meaning was there for all to hear without the need to resort to a written text. Although by no means the most subtle of Mahler's early symphonies, the '*Resurrection's*' spiritual fervour and almost continual panoply of spine-tingling invention, has ensured its popularity to the present day.

Meanwhile, and despite certain reservations, Mahler agreed to sign a new five-year contract at Hamburg, although in the end he would only see three of them through. It was about now that he also first came into contact with the budding young conductor Bruno Walter (then Schlesinger), who started out as chorus master, but the following year found himself rapidly promoted to the position of assistant conductor. In addition, Mahler was developing a close relationship with Richard Strauss. The two budding composers had been running a kind of mutual admiration society for some time, intuitively aware that in German-speaking circles theirs were the most important and individual post-Wagnerian creative talents. For a while there was even the distinct possibility that Strauss would come to work at Hamburg. The two gave each other a great deal of support, and although Mahler's attempts to stage Strauss's early opera, *Guntrum*, in Hamburg eventually came to nothing, Strauss was successful in organizing a performance of Mahler's '*Titan*' in Weimar on 3 June.

The 1894–95 season saw Mahler return to regular concert hall work with a season of eight concerts with the Hamburg Philharmonic, including a performance of Beethoven's *Ninth Symphony* that left the audience stunned, if not entirely for all the right reasons. Mahler lived in an age when the score of a great composer was not considered sacrosanct. Conductors had free rein to alter the scoring, and make any 'necessary' cuts, according to their taste. Mahler's increased confidence both as a conductor and a composer led him, on this occasion, to tinker around with Beethoven's original a great deal, not only bolstering the brass section, but going as far as to place the military band offstage for the famous section in the finale accompanying the solo tenor. He had, in effect, 'Mahlerized' the great work with the most sincere of intentions. However, this was not quite what the directors of the Hamburg Philharmonic originally had in mind, and the next year Mahler was promptly replaced by Felix Weingartner. His spirits were at least raised by a concert in Berlin, during which Richard Strauss had arranged for him to conduct the first three movements of the *Second Symphony* on 4 March 1895. This was, in effect, a trial run for the complete symphony later in the year.

Meanwhile, Mahler was attempting to put his private life in order. On 6 February, his brother Otto shot himself, but despite Mahler's typically pained reaction at the news of the death of his familial favourite, he rather untypically responded by determining to make more of his own life. During the spring of 1895 he moved into new accommodation in the Parkallee with his sisters Justine and Emma. This handsome, third-floor apartment became the scene of innumerable chamber music evenings, which Mahler arranged with close friends, and which helped to offset the frustrations of his regular work. Mahler adored these informal sessions, and amazed his friends with how intact his piano technique was after years of serious neglect. In addition, he took up cycling – a craze current craze in Hamburg at the time.

His spirits raised by these non-curricular activities, Mahler began work on his *Third Symphony* that summer at Steinbach. He originally intended to cast it in a lighter vein, but typically his ideas emerged on the grandest of possible scales – another of Mahler's 'entire worlds'. The work was planned in seven movements, although he finally settled on only six, the jettisoned movement becoming the finale of the *Fourth Symphony*. It seems that he had most of it completed by the end of the summer, except for the first movement. Most interestingly we learn from Bauer-Lechner, Mahler's cycling companion that summer, about his attitude towards the genre of the 'symphony' as a whole:

> *Perhaps one shouldn't really call it a 'symphony' as it hardly conforms to the normal formal outlines. But then the word 'symphony' suggests to me the building of a whole world with every possible means available at my disposal. The ideas and the way they are used dictate their overall form. As a result with each new work I go back to basics in effect so that my inspiration*

> *can be freely taken where it needs to go, even though I always feel in complete control.*

From now on, Mahler invariably spent the summer months composing, and the conducting season working on revisions during his spare time.

During 1895, Mahler also made the acquaintance of the soprano Anna von Mildenburg, whom he trained and clearly felt a great kinship with. She became one of his closest friends and correspondents up to the time of his departure from Hamburg in 1897.

The winter season of 1895 was highlighted by Mahler conducting the world premiere of his complete *Second Symphony* in Berlin on 13 December. It scored an enormous public and critical success, securing once and for all Mahler's reputation as a serious composer. Another Berlin concert in March of the following year, featuring movements from the *First* and *Second Symphonies* and a selection of songs, was less enthusiastically received, although at least one member of the audience was deeply moved – one Arthur Nikisch, who there and then expressed a desire to conduct some of Mahler's music himself.

While impatiently waiting for the sketches of his *Third Symphony* to arrive – he had forgetfully left them in Hamburg – Mahler began the summer composing one of his most exuberant *Wunderhorn* songs, '*Lob des Verstandes*'. Then he gave his individual attention to the work that he most fervently believed in.

The *Third Symphony* is the one most bound up with Mahler's feelings about the natural world, 'awakened', as he put it, 'from mysterious silence into glorious sounds. . . . ' He explained in a letter that the *Third* has nothing whatsoever to do with an individual's struggles (unlike its two predecessors), more the path of nature. The movement's titles had been added after the music had formulated in his mind – the reason for his later decision to remove them. These were as follows: (I) 'Pan's Awakening' or 'Summer Marches in' (later, 'The Procession of Bacchus'), (II) 'What the Flowers of the Fields Tell Me', (III) 'What the Animals of the Forest Tell Me', (IV) 'What the Night Tells Me' (later 'What Man Tells Me'), (V) 'What the Cuckoo Tells Me' (later 'Morning Bells'), and (VI) 'What Love Tells Me'. He was utterly convinced of the symphony's worth as he went along:

My symphony will be something the world has never heard before. In it Nature herself acquires a voice and tells secrets so profound that they are perhaps glimpsed only in dreams! I assure you, there are passages where I myself get a most peculiar feeling, almost as though it was not I who had composed them.

Far from being intimidated by the vast scale of its predecessor, Mahler went one stage further with the two-part *Third Symphony*. It lasts nearly an hour and three-quarters, the first movement spanning an incredible thirty-five minutes, forming Part I on its own. This stunning, march-style creation possesses an inexorable, brooding power, which appears to propel itself along effortlessly. The final dash to the finishing post is one of the most exuberantly uncomplicated passages Mahler ever penned.

Given the scale of the glorious finale – a ravishing twenty-five-minute slow movement of skin-tingling sensitivity – the outer movements tend to be experienced like a pair of gargantuan bookends, between which the other four act as multifaceted interludes: a blissfully contented *Tempo di Menuetto*, a lusty *scherzando* of joyful rusticity, a deeply-felt meditation for solo contralto on the midnight song from Nietzsche's *Also sprach Zarathustra*, and an utterly enchanting women's/children's chorus, '*Bimm, Bamm!*'. Even though once again Mahler fills the symphonic cooking pot up to the rim with a whole range of seemingly incompatible ingredients, the whole thing somehow gels together magnificently. Despite its awesome scale, the mastery of touch throughout is such that the listener is almost invariably left with the surprising sensation that everything has somehow passed by in the twinkling of an eye.

Mahler's reputation at the opera house had meanwhile taken something of a downturn. The conservative element was getting the upper hand, complaining that Mahler was spending far too much time worrying about his own 'questionable' compositions and orchestral concerts than he was about the opera house. The Manager, Pollini, responded by going out of his way to make circumstances as uncomfortable as possible for Mahler, principally by hiring a second conductor, and then giving the latter some of Mahler's favourite scores to conduct – Wagner's *Tristan und Isolde* and *Die Meistersinger*. Mahler, for his part, appears to have resigned himself to the situation, and was in any case more distracted at the time by his composing than anything else. In addition, he had his eye on the job as conductor of the Vienna court opera, where the health of the current holder of the post was causing some concern. There were objections – not the least of which was his Jewishness – but Mahler pulled in all the friends and contacts he had built up over the years to intercede on his behalf and recommend him for the post. Even Brahms, whom Mahler faithfully visited over the last two years of his life, threw in a sincere vote of confidence. Meanwhile, applications for posts in Berlin, Munich and Dresden had been turned down, also because of his religious background.

The Vienna situation was only finally resolved when the appropriate authorities were notified that Mahler had adopted the Christian faith, having been officially baptized as a Catholic just before leaving Hamburg on 23 February 1897. This essentially gave him his entrée into the Austrian capital, and at the beginning of April he formally accepted the offer of a post, due initially to run for one year from 1 June. Vienna was to be his musical base for the next ten years.

CHAPTER 5

EUROPE'S NEW MUSIC DIRECTOR
(1897–1902)

- ◆ Anti-Semitism
- ◆ First major opera productions
- ◆ The Vienna Philharmonic
- ◆ Rückert Lieder
- ◆ Fourth and Fifth Symphonies
- ◆ Marriage, and birth of first daughter

The eyes of the musical world now fell upon Gustav Mahler, yet he was still regarded with a great deal of suspicion by the local Viennese population. An article in the *Reichspost* dated 14 April 1897 highlights the situation with startling clarity:

> *That fact that he [Mahler] was showered with praise by the Budapest newspapers is proof enough of his origins. We, of course, will give him every chance to prove himself. The Jewish papers have their champion for the time being, but only the fullness of time will reveal whether this Jew-boy will prove worthy of such acclaim or will find himself brushed aside when reality strikes.*

Mahler's debut production on 10 May was Wagner's *Lohengrin*, a highly demanding work lasting in the region of 3½ hours, for which he was allowed only one rehearsal. Clearly he had his work cut out to get it ready in time, although from the word go, he knew that, musically at least, he was in the right place. As he told Natalie Bauer-Lechner:

> *I can do anything with this orchestra. After just one rehearsal they had achieved a standard which would have taken years with some outfits. . . . Their greatest assets are their unequalled musicianship, and their sheer natural ability, combined with extraordinary warmth and sheer enthusiasm.*

Lohengrin scored an immediate success. Mahler virtually had Vienna eating out of his hands overnight – suddenly his ultimate goal of becoming overall director seemed less of a pipe dream. Over the following week (imagine anyone undertaking such a schedule nowadays) he directed sensational performances of *Die Walküre*, *Siegfried*, *The Marriage of Figaro* and *The Magic Flute*. He could hardly have chosen a more risky combination than Mozart and Wagner with which to establish his Viennese reputation, but in the event, the gamble paid off handsomely. Such was his extraordinary impact that Mahler was appointed Deputy-Director in July, and then, following the ill health of the current post-holder, was appointed Director on 8 September with almost autonomous powers, a healthy salary of 13,000 florins, and a guaranteed 3,000 florins a year for life whenever he decided to leave.

Mahler found himself some comfortable, fully-furnished lodgings near the University and moved in with his sisters Justine and Emma. He also struck up a close friendship with Arnold Rosé, who led the opera orchestra for an unprecedented period of fifty years. In 1898, Mahler's sister Emma married Arnold's brother Eduard, a cellist in the Boston Symphony Orchestra, and in 1902 Arnold followed suit by marrying Justine.

The summer of 1897 was spent in the Tyrol, where he convalesced after a severe bout of tonsillitis. However, for Mahler and his immediate circle, the main concern was the strong possibility that Anna von Mildenburg was coming to sing with the Vienna Opera. It would seem that he had an all-engulfing passion for Anna. Part of his reason for leaving Hamburg in the first place was that he had become so obsessed with her that he found it impossible to maintain his usual professional stance when she was in the cast. That summer, she received several letters from Mahler and his friends begging her not to come, or failing that, pleading with her to follow the strictest guidelines in terms of her day-to-day contact with Mahler. Although she still came, she appears to have handled the situation with great sensitivity. Mahler dedicated his *Das klagende Lied* to her out of sincere appreciation.

Another double-edged friendship also reared its head at this time with the great composer of *Lieder*, Hugo Wolf, who was by now was on the verge of a nervous collapse. Things began well enough, with Mahler making every effort to put on a production of Wolf's opera *Der Corregidor*, and Wolf, for his part, waxing lyrical about Mahler's production of Wagner's *Ring* cycle in the autumn. However, following a totally fatuous disagreement over Rubinstein's opera *The Demon* – hardly a masterpiece, but one for which Mahler harboured considerable affection – everything turned sour, and Wolf was finally pushed over the edge. He was reported to be ranting and raving, and became so violent that he had to be physically restrained. Mahler, for his part, eventually got *Der Corregidor* produced, but despite his best efforts it failed to gain a foothold in the regular performing repertoire.

Controversy seemed to follow Mahler wherever he went. His first production of the new 1897–98 season, Dvořák's *Dalibor*, proved no exception, and unwittingly caused something of an uproar in the press. At this time, the Austrian Empire still extended as far as Moravia and Bohemia, and there had been moves afoot recently to allow the native languages of these territories supremacy over the imposed German tongue. In such an atmosphere, Mahler's production took on political implications that did nothing to recommend him to members of the anti-Jewish/anti-Czech community. Nevertheless, his position was, for the time being, almost unassailable. He was the talk of the city, and had already overtaken his colleague at the opera, the great Hans Richter, in most people's affections. Even the Emperor sought an audience with Mahler in order to congratulate him on the extraordinary impact he had made in such a short space of time.

The only problem was that Mahler was so busy that, as he put it, 'there's simply no time for "working" (i.e., composing).' At least he received a boost on the creative front when on 3 March 1898 he conducted a Prague Philharmonic performance of his *First Symphony*, which won a standing ovation from the capacity audience. The start of the season also witnessed two events of great importance. Mahler gave the first performance of Wagner's

Ring outside Bayreuth, which was complete in every way, with all the traditionally-cut material reinstated. The other was a totally unexpected invitation to take over at the helm of the Vienna Philharmonic following Richter's resignation. So colourful was his tenure that it might be as well to give here a brief outline of his term of office, which ended somewhat abruptly in April 1901.

The Vienna Philharmonic, as now, was drawn from players on the roster of the court opera, so they were already familiar with their 'new' conductor. Yet away from the exacting disciplines of the opera pit, many of the players were upset by Mahler's notoriously high standards, and desire for technical perfection. Another problem was his conducting technique – vastly different from the majestic sweep of Richter. Mahler was fidgety, even angular, in his movements, continually responsive to each tiny detail rather than making broad gestures. In the opera pit this passed virtually unnoticed, but with all eyes focused on him, it gave the newspapers something of a field day.

In addition, Mahler was in the habit of 'improving' scores with a 'composer's ear'. An added E flat clarinet in Beethoven's *'Coriolan' Overture* was promptly removed in future performances in response to one critical hammer blow, and his 'transcription' of Beethoven's Op. 132 *String Quartet in A minor* for a full complement of strings also made the purists' blood boil. His usual habit of using an off-stage orchestra in the finale of the *Ninth Symphony*, as well as touching up the orchestration here and there, proved particularly unwelcome, even from normally supportive critics. Nevertheless, the *audiences* were apparently in awe for the most part, relishing the stunning clarity and impact of his performances, the result of his insistence on thorough rehearsals for even the most familiar pieces by Mozart and Beethoven.

Over the following three years, Mahler conducted a vast range of repertoire, including works by his friend Richard Strauss (a mesmerizing *Aus Italien*), and acclaimed performances of Bruckner's *Fifth* and *Sixth Symphonies*, the latter the work's premiere, given on 26 February 1899. He also directed his own *First* and *Second Symphonies*, although the conservative Viennese audience could make little sense of the latter. One of Mahler's many young female admirers was one of the promenaders at the Viennese premiere of the *First Symphony* on 18 November 1900. Having described the usual riotous behaviour that invariably accompanied such occasions – shades of Harrison Birtwistle in our own time – she recollected:

> *Only the youngest stood firm in the ear-splitting din which followed each movement, totally in awe of that intense bespectacled man, and clapped and roared our applause until we were hoarse. . . . We rushed to the rostrum ecstatically calling out Mahler's name leaving the 'opposition' jeering behind us . . . I will never forget the look of anguish which lay behind the gentle smile with which he greeted our applause. . . .*

Mahler also directed performances of his *Lieder eines fahrenden Gesellen* and some of the *Wunderhorn* songs. Writing of the latter, the great Viennese critic Eduard Hanslick perceptively commented:

> *There is an innate dichotomy between the gentle inspiration of 'folk music' and a modern, sophisticated orchestral accompaniment. Yet Mahler has somehow managed to combine the two with astonishing mastery and the greatest subtlety. With every new work which appears from the pens of Mahler, Strauss and Wolf, as we enter the new millennia, one feels increasingly sure that the future must surely be theirs.*

Mahler also took the orchestra on a successful tour of Paris in June 1900 as part of the International Exhibition there to mark the new century. Pierre Lalo in *Le Temps* noted:

> *Here in France our conductors hardly spare any attention to the music of the great masters at all. Mahler is typical of German [sic] conductors in that he pays too much attention to detail. For him almost every note carries with it its own meaning of great significance. . . .*

All the time, Mahler's strict discipline was increasingly at odds with the orchestra's laid-back temperament. Matters came to a head early in 1901 when, following a haemorrhage, he was forced to take a break in the Adriatic. While he was away, the orchestra's committee made their move. Well aware that Mahler's contract was up for renewal in the September, they appointed in his place the decidedly mediocre Joseph Hellmesberger, the young assistant conductor of the opera's ballet company. Deeply upset, Mahler handed in his resignation in the April, a decision which, ironically, he had more-or-less already come to on his own as he could no longer cope with the demands of running both the opera and the Philharmonic concerts.

To return to the summer of 1899, Mahler's vacation at Bad Aussee in the Salzkammergut was proving creatively unproductive, with nothing more than a couple of *Wunderhorn* settings put down. These included the popular '*Revelge*' (Reveille), a militaristic setting that was to provide the starting point for the opening movement of the *Sixth Symphony*. It was only shortly before leaving for Vienna that ideas at last began to stir for a large-scale work – his *Fourth Symphony*. We learn from Bauer-Lechner that Mahler was creatively excited in a way that he had not been since *Das klagende Lied*. However, Vienna beckoned once more.

Bauer-Lechner and Justine Mahler were so concerned at Mahler's plight that they took it upon themselves to find a suitable place where he might compose undisturbed the following summer. They visited the Wörthersee, where Brahms composed many of his late works. Having made contact with an architect named Theuer, Mahler made a swift trip from Vienna to give the place his approval and to find an isolated spot in some woods near Maiernigg where the villa was to be built.

The 1899–1900 schedule was particularly hectic, due to Mahler's continuing dual role between the opera house and the Philharmonic. In February 1900, Hans Richter resigned his post due to failing health, leaving Mahler the undisputed principal conductor of Vienna and the anti-Mahler faction blaming the composer directly for Richter's departure.

The season was crowned by sensational performances of Bizet's *Carmen*, although by now, what Mahler most looked forward to was the thought of getting back to Maiernigg and doing serious work on the *Fourth Symphony* during the summer. Things did not, however, get off to a very good start, according to Natalie Bauer-Lechner:

> *He was decidedly on edge, bordering on despair, saying that he had dried up, and that having gone to all the trouble of having built a house specially for him to compose in, he wouldn't be able to think of anything.*

When Mahler finally got going, he could hardly stem the flow of white-hot inspiration – he worked between six and ten hours a day until the symphony was nearly complete. It required just a little touching up, which helped to keep his mind occupied during the arduous new opera season.

The *Fourth* is Mahler's most compact, classically aware, sparsely orchestrated, and popular symphony. Cast in the traditional four movements, with the *Ländler*/scherzo second, the whole work lasts in the region of fifty-five minutes, which, along with the *First*, makes it one of only two Mahler symphonies to clock in at less than an hour. It is also the one symphony that reverses the normal psychological process of triumph in the face of adversity. The generally bright and breezy first movement – a piece of almost nonchalant, formal complexity – is resolved in the childlike innocence of the finale, the *Wunderhorn* setting, '*Das himmlische Leben*' ('Heavenly life'), which had been rejected from the *Third Symphony*.

The scherzo is a comparatively easy-going affair, although Mahlerian irony rears its head in the form of a specially tuned (*scorditura*) solo violin representing death in the time-honoured manner of Saint-Saëns's *Danse macabre*. Yet the humour is no more than mildly unsettling, especially when compared with the chilling intensity of its later symphonic cousins. The untroubled spiritual serenity of the slow movement achieves a sublimity of expression that Mahler would never fully recapture. The passage where the gates of heaven finally open appears to make time stand still as we bask in the sunshine of a radiant E major eruption, the perfect preparation for the blissfully inspired finale, Mahler's enraptured swansong to the symphonies of his *Wunderhorn* period.

The winter season was alleviated by a celebrated performance of Mahler's *Second Symphony* in Munich during October for the local Hugo Wolf Society. During the celebrations afterwards he was reported by a fellow guest, Ludwig Schiedermair, to have commented excitedly on programme music (i.e., that which tells a story) in a way that has a fascinating bearing on his own music:

> *Programmes should not be allowed as they raise false expectations. Let the public make up their own minds, and don't distract them with unnecessary images when they should be listening. If a composer manages to convey the feelings that led him to write*

the music in the first place then he will have succeeded entirely. In that case, music has come close to verbal expression, but has conveyed far more than the mere word ever can.

Another major event during the first half of the season was the hiring of the legendary tenor, Leo Slezak (1873–1946), who later recalled in 1922 the profound effect Mahler had on this period in his career. Having extolled the virtues of Mahler's legendary Mozart productions, which – in their restoring of recitatives, harpsichord and integration of production, music, design and costumes – set the standard for the new century, he continued:

It wouldn't even occur to any of us to take a rest during rehearsals when Mahler was doing a scene which didn't concern our particular character. . . . He had this extraordinary ability to inspire us to give our all.

As the season went on, Mahler became increasingly frustrated by the pull between his conducting and composing. At least the two came together again on 17 February with the premiere of *Das klagende Lied*, now some twenty years old. Critics were on the whole lukewarm in their appreciation, and in some quarters the inevitable anti-Mahlerian attitudes still prevailed. These were typified by Josef Scheu's waspish comment in the *Workers' Paper* of 24 February: 'Remember the kind of thing Karl Löwe managed with this kind of material! And all he required was one singer and a piano. . . .'

Following his illness and the Philharmonic debacle in the spring of 1901, Mahler was delighted to secure the services of Bruno Walter as second conductor at the Opera, before heading for Maiernigg-am-Wörthersee and composition. Once again we owe it to Bauer-Lechner's documentary-like recollections of these creative summers that we have any idea what Mahler was up to on such occasions. He was notoriously disorganized in this respect, and often even forgot to date his letters.

That summer Mahler composed several new songs, taking two days over each – one to compose, another to orchestrate. These comprised a new *Wunderhorn* setting, the first three *Kindertotenlieder* (the last two settings followed in 1904) and the first four of the five *Rückert Lieder*, completed the following summer.

These initially appeared in print as '*Seven Lieder*', the first two being a pair of Wunderhorn settings: the '*Revelge*', and a deeply moving funeral march, '*Der Tambourg'sell*' (The drummer boy).

Mahler described the magical first song '*Ich atmet' einen Linden Duft*' ('I breathed a fragrance soft and sweet') as engendering the kind of feeling one experiences in the company of someone with whom there is such a natural empathy that words become unnecessary. The parallel with his initial encounter with Alma later that same year need hardly be emphasized. He was less sure, however, about '*Blicke mir nicht in die Lieder*' ('Do not try to read my songs!'), whose more relaxed atmosphere he cynically thought would almost certainly guarantee its success. '*Um Mitternacht*' ('At midnight') is one of Mahler's most hauntingly unforgiving inspirations, while '*Liebst du um Schönheit*' ('If thou lovest beauty') and '*Ich bin der Welt abhanden gekommen*' ('I have become a stranger to the world') both hint strongly at the sighing suspensions that were to reach their apex in the beloved *Adagietto* of the *Fifth Symphony*.

Perhaps of even greater significance was the formulation in Mahler's mind and initial sketches for the *Fifth Symphony*:

> *It would be quite inappropriate to use voices here. There is no need for words as everything can be expressed in purely instrumental terms. I've planned it as a typical symphonic structure in four movements, each an independent whole which exhibits a sense of 'belonging' only in terms of its general mood.*

Returning to Vienna, the beginning of the new season was marked by the first public appearance of Bruno Walter on 28 September at the helm of Verdi's *Aida*. Walter's indebtedness to Mahler's distinctive gesturing was noted, although it was accounted a successful debut all round.

The most important – indeed crucial – event in Mahler's personal life occurred during November at a party given by Berta Zuckerkandl, a keen supporter of new artistic movements in Vienna, including, of course, Mahler's own music. Here he met for the very first time, the gifted, beautiful and high-spirited Alma, daughter of the great painter Anton Schindler. She was a talented pianist and promising composer in her own right, then studying under Alexander von Zemlinsky. Mahler was transfixed by her presence from the start, according to Alma's own recollections of the occasion:

> *We had splintered away from the main group . . . and were enjoying that special aura that surrounds two people who have just 'connected'. I assured him that I 'would visit at whatever point I had something worth showing him.' He looked slightly disappointed commenting that this 'could take quite some time'.*

Nevertheless Mahler at least managed to get an assurance out of her to attend his first new production of the season – Offenbach's *The Tales of Hofmann* – hardly staple Mahlerian fayre, but rehearsed and performed with the meticulousness and enthusiasm he would have accorded one of the great classics. The relationship blossomed fast and furiously, fuelled by Mahler's almost claustrophobic fixation. During November he wrote to her enclosing published editions of all his songs inscribed to her. Later the same month, during a touching stroll in the snows around Vienna, he proposed to her, not formally, but apparently simply by talking in a way that seemed to assume that their destiny lay together.

Contemporaneously, Mahler was busy making preparations for the first performances of the *Fourth Symphony*. The Munich premiere on 25 November 1901 was less than well received, although a performance in Berlin on 16 December, conducted by Mahler as part of a concert otherwise directed by Richard Strauss, established the work's early popularity. Strauss was quite in awe of the new work, particularly the *Adagio*, which he admitted, with a self-effacing modesty quite untypical of the headstrong young German, he could not possibly have written himself. In homage, he sent Mahler a parcel of his complete published works.

Mahler's overwhelming obsession with Alma is illustrated by an extraordinary and totally unreasonable demand made in their correspondence of the period. She had written to him apologizing for her delay as she had had some exercises to do for Zemlinsky. Mahler was so hurt that she apparently felt her composing to be more important than writing to him that he forbade her to compose any more. Although desperately upset at first, it seems – incredibly – that she acceded to this utterly breathtaking demand of absolute loyalty.

The new year was highlighted by the first two performances

of the *Fourth Symphony* in Vienna conducted by Mahler with the Philharmonic. Even the usual doubters appear to have been gagged by this most economical and restrained of all the symphonies. Sadly, his attempts to do his bit for Richard Strauss failed dismally, for his meticulously rehearsed and directed production of Strauss' early opera *Feuersnot* was met by such hostile press and public reaction that he was forced to take it off after only three performances.

On 9 March, Mahler and Alma Schindler were married after a courtship lasting only four months, and for their honeymoon made a trip to St Petersburg, where Mahler had been invited to direct a number of concerts. By some extraordinary coincidence, Mahler's sister, Justine, was married to Arnold Rosé the very next day. The temperature was unbelievably cold at that time of year and the River Neva was frozen over – in the afternoons, the town's population would take to the ice. The concerts were a great success, Mahler's performances of Beethoven's '*Eroica*' and Mozart's late *G minor Symphony* (both specialities of his) bringing special praise for their clear-headedness and sparkling originality.

Meanwhile, the creative side of things continued to look up to an extent hardly dreamt of only a couple of years before. The *Third Symphony* at last received its complete premiere in Krefeld, and scored such a roaring success that the audience had to be controlled by Strauss, who had immediately gone up on stage to congratulate Mahler publicly after the performance. Alma, who had sat alone in the audience that night, was so overcome by what she recognized as the 'sheer genius' of the work that she knew that from then on she wanted only to devote herself completely to its creator. Over the years, the age difference between the two, and Mahler's stubborn insistence that she totally subsume her entire existence to his career, put increasing strain on the relationship. But for now, everything was blissful contentment.

The summer was of the greatest importance to Mahler, for at least he could finish work on the abandoned *Fifth Symphony*, two movements of which had been virtually completed the previous summer. It is often grouped with the *Sixth* and *Seventh Symphonies* as a purely instrumental triumvirate that use predominantly the *Rückert Lieder* as a resource for musical ideas – although there are still obvious references to both the '*Wunderhorn*' songs and the *Kindertotenlieder*. For all three, Mahler declined the use of any kind of literary programme. He still employed a huge orchestra with all kinds of exotic instrumentation (cowbells in the *Sixth*, a guitar and mandolin in the *Seventh*), although the chamber-scale delicacy and contrapuntal complexity of much of the writing is in marked contrast to their predecessors. Most importantly, there is a new macabre intensity to the writing, a penchant for the mysterious, which contrasts markedly with the emotional directness of Mahler's existing music.

The *Fifth Symphony* is in five movements, which travel in tonality from C sharp minor to D major, this time divided into three parts, two outer pairings and a whiplash central Scherzo-Burleske of phenomenal virtuoso drive and searing intensity. The first is a funeral march with two contrasting trio sections whose material is then transformed into a second movement of a disturbingly brutal, 'stormy' (Mahler's word) nature. The music on the other side of the Burleske is emotionally far more conventional, but no less masterly in its handling. The famous *Adagietto*, with its heart-tugging chains of suspensions and sequences, leads directly to one of the most unashamedly forthright and positive movements in any of the symphonies. However, beneath the untroubled exterior of this extraordinary Rondo finale lies a wealth of creative ingenuity in the way of thematic cross-referencing and fertilization. Mahler had at last joined the great masters whose most profound achievements so often lie hidden from view.

Alma proved herself to be of invaluable help in copying out the parts of the *Fifth Symphony* as Mahler went along – as the summer progressed she became more and more used to his shorthand. For Mahler, these were possibly the most perfectly contented few months of his life, highlighted by the birth of his first daughter, Maria Anna, on 3 November. He was to grow very close to little 'Putzi', as he affectionately called her – they would spend hours together, just the two of them, talking and playing. She only had eyes for her father, whose determined personality she inherited. Little did anyone know that Maria would not live to see her fifth birthday.

CHAPTER 6
COMPOSER OR CONDUCTOR?
(1902–7)

- ♦ *International appearances as conductor/composer*
- ♦ *Kindertotenlieder*
- ♦ *Symphonies Nos.6–8*
- ♦ *Friendship with Richard Strauss*
- ♦ *Support for Schoenberg*
- ♦ *Death of María*

Mahler's high technical standards and revolutionary integration of all aspects of operatic production reached a new level during the 1902–3 season. He had become friendly with a group of progressive artists of various persuasions collectively referred to as the Vienna Secessionists, and had invited a prominent member, the painter Alfred Roller, to oversee all aspects of stage design at the Vienna Opera.

Their first production together was Wagner's *Tristan und Isolde* in February 1903, throughout which Roller's impressionistic use of colour created a sensation. The play of light and shade, and the way the scenes seemed to grow out of one another (helped by subtle use of the curtains), added a further psychological dimension to the music-drama being played out on stage.

Another event during February was of a less happy kind – Hugo Wolf's funeral. Wolf had been such a headstrong, self-opinionated and irascible character that he had endeared himself to very few people, even prior to his nervous breakdown. His passing appears to have had a profoundly melancholic effect on all those who attended. The sense of loss was heightened by the feeling that something should have been done to help prevent the innovative song-writer's appalling demise.

During April, Mahler gained permission to conduct a concert of his own works in Lembach, including his *First Symphony*. The orchestra had been superbly prepared technically, but were musically clearly out of their depth. Mahler wrote to Alma despairingly: 'On several occasions I was reduced to a cold sweat. For crying out loud, what kind of musical sensitivities must these people possess if they can't even understand *this*?'

Rather more auspicious was a gala performance of the *Second Symphony*, given in the awe-inspiring surroundings of Basle Cathedral on 15 June. He spent several days rehearsing the chorus and orchestra, who had already been meticulously prepared by the musical director there. The result was the most celebrated of all early performances of the symphony. The Basle *National Zeitung* was ecstatic:

> *It would be difficult to praise too highly this performance. Indeed, we have never heard the like of it from our admittedly vastly expanded orchestra, and Mahler's direction can only be described as the work of a genius. . . . When was the last time we heard a* pianissimo *like that from our choral society?*

Most interestingly, as part of the same review, the paper mentions Mahler's conducting style as the very model of composure, noting that it was 'free of any extraneous gestures'. Perhaps the luxury of innumerable pre-concert rehearsals meant that there had been no need for Mahler to resort to his usual range of impassioned pleas in order to compensate for less-than-satisfactory preparation time.

The summer was marked by a welcome return to the idyllic surroundings of Maiernigg, although the usual symphonic frustrations quickly resurfaced. He managed to complete two movements of the monumental *Sixth Symphony*, but with detailed ideas already formulating in his mind for the remainder, he simply ran out of time. These composing 'breaks' at Mahler's private retreat invariably saw him in a more relaxed frame of mind away from the hubbub of city life. He was an early riser and would often go for an early-morning dip in the lake before 6am. After breakfast he worked solidly for about seven hours until taking a late lunch, and then would go for a walk in the woods with Alma. The evenings were spent reading to each other, when Mahler might indulge in a cigar and a beer – though never to excess. He was also a hearty sleeper.

While Mahler was away on holiday, the orchestra pit at the Vienna opera had been altered following his own strict instructions. It was lowered over a foot-and-a-half, thereby making the orchestra's presence far less distracting for the audience, and also subtly reducing the impact of the sound they made. In addition, he had the playing area expanded by about fifteen square yards to facilitate another of his little revolutions – from now on, the principal string players would sit close to him, with the rest of the orchestra fanning out in all directions, making the conductor the focal point of attention.

The 1903–4 season was marked by several concerts with other orchestras, which serve to underline Mahler's near-celebrity status by this time, both as composer and conductor. In late October he directed both his *First* and *Third Symphonies* with the Concertgebouw Orchestra in Amsterdam. Mahler was overjoyed with the great Dutch orchestra, then in the capable hands of Willem Mengelberg. The latter became a devoted and skilful interpreter of Mahler's works, indeed the only conductor to whom Mahler felt he could entrust his precious music with complete confidence.

During February 1904, Mahler took the *Third Symphony*, which was fast establishing itself as his most popular work, to both Mannheim and Heidelberg. Once again, both Mahler and the audience were unusually enthusiastic about the results. Although the anti-Semitic element in Vienna was becoming an increasing problem, Mahler was riding on the crest of a wave of international success. Even Viennese officialdom gave him its formal seal of approval when the Emperor Franz Joseph I presented Mahler with the Order of the Iron Cross (third class) in recognition of his achievements.

As the season came to a close, Mahler became the official symbol of Vienna's composers when he was appointed Honorary President of the newly formed Viennese Association of Creative Musicians. Other members included Arnold Schoenberg, Alexander Zemlinsky (an almost fanatical admirer of Mahler's), and Bruno Walter. Mahler was increasingly drawn into this circle of radicals – Berg and Webern would soon join their number – who saw Mahler as their natural spiritual leader. Mahler did not always see eye-to-eye with their music, but passionately stood up for what they were trying to achieve, admitting that although this might not be the route for him, it was in all probability where the future of music really lay. By the end of his life, he, too, was on the brink of abandoning tonality – he had effectively arrived at the same place but by a different method and at a different time.

The summer got off to a wonderful start with the birth of Mahler's second daughter, Anna Justina, on 15 July. She was destined to become a distinguished sculptress, and the wife of two highly distinguished musicians, first the composer Ernst Krenek, and later the conductor Anatole Fistoulari.

Mahler's principal aim that summer was to complete his *Sixth Symphony*. Time was therefore at a premium. He simply had no choice but to leave mother and newly-born daughter and make his way swiftly to Maiernigg. The vacation was a particularly happy one, but despite Mahler's generally high spirits, the music he was writing of was of a profoundly uncompromising, often tragic hue. This was in all probability intensified by the appalling stormy weather that hit the area during the first half of the vacation. He began with two new songs to add to the three of 1901, which together comprise his *Kindertotenlieder* ('Songs on the death of children'), once again based on the poems of Friedrich Rückert, who had originally written them in response to the tragedy of losing two of his own children.

Given the happiness of the recent birth and Mahler's devotion to his eldest daughter, there is a macabre slant to all this. Mahler later claimed that he had written them in case such a thing should happen – and cruelly, it did.

Throughout, Mahler handles his material with a divine mastery. Despite the profound intensity of feeling that brought them into being in the first place, the music never overheats in the manner of some of his other work, nor relies on overtly tuneful material – more a profound lyricism. There is a calm and noble acceptance that rises far above mere neurosis and heightened emotionalism. The orchestration is sparse (no heavy brass, only two horns), the atmosphere almost magical despite the subject matter, as exemplified by the haunting *'Nun will die Sonn' so hell aufgeh'n'* ('Once more the sun will dawn so bright'). The whole cycle is transfigured by the final '*In diesem Wetter, in diesem Braus*' ('In such weather, in such tumult'), which seeks to resolve worldly concerns and tensions by the touch of God's hand.

Mahler immediately set to work on the remainder of his *Sixth Symphony*. Alma Mahler gives some fascinating insights into what lay behind some of the most inspired music Mahler ever penned. Having explained that the first movement's elated second theme was intended as a portrait of herself, she continues:

> *The third movement contains a passage suggestive of children playing in the sand . . . their shouting gradually takes on a more sinister hue, until at the end the whole thing simply expires. The finale is a self-portrait of sorts, in which Mahler in heroic mould anticipates his own destruction. . . .*

The *Sixth* is the most galvanizingly 'physical' of all Mahler's symphonies, the most unrelenting in its expression of the dark side of human existence. It also appears to have been a form of exorcism, a necessary emotional journey, which, although it terrified Mahler, had to be undertaken – the late works could never have been written without it. He was plagued by self-doubts during the rehearsals, and was so transfixed by its inexorable power that he only got through the premiere with the greatest of difficulty. His doubts and neuroses even extended to reversing the order of the two central movements for a while.

As it stands, this four-movement work is one of the most hair-raising symphonic edifices ever created. A turbulently thrusting first movement is as clear-cut formally as the *Fourth's* equivalent, yet here the doom-laden atmosphere is like nothing ever encountered in the music of the classical era. The gentle sound of cowbells and an ending in the major key provide only temporary respite from the general angst. The scherzo similarly transforms the usual Mahlerian *Ländler* into a sequence of malevolent grotesquerie in which potentially innocent material continually takes on a more sinister hue.

If the heavenly *Andante moderato* third movement provides the work's only spiritual resting place, the finale plunges us right back into the abyss. Opening with a dismal cry for help, this vast movement is punctuated by hammer-blows of fate, thrashed out by the timpani. This time there is no major key affirmation, merely a descent into total despair and hopelessness.

Mahler then rounded off this most extraordinarily productive of all his summers at Maiernigg by sketching out the two '*Nachtmusik*' movements of the *Seventh Symphony*.

The new Vienna season got off to tremendous start with a new production of *Fidelio*, featuring Alfred Roller's stunningly inventive designs and lighting. Uppermost in Mahler's mind, however, was the forthcoming premiere of his *Fifth Symphony* in Cologne on 18 October. The preparations went extremely well – the highly-exacting composer excitedly reported in a letter to Alma that the orchestra was 'first rate!' Yet, particularly in the third movement, this is the most contrapuntally active of all the symphonies, with all sorts of instrumental lines busily interweaving and interrelating simultaneously. It was this aspect of the score that mitigated against its success in the press, and even the normally supportive Bruno Walter admitted to a certain sense of frustration at the lack of clarity in the instrumentation. Mahler was only too well aware of these defects and eventually made a thorough revision of the score with this very much in mind. Although these days we may almost take this symphony for granted, at the time it was considered a very tough nut to crack, its strange blend of heavy nostalgia, brooding melancholy and biting cynicism presenting all sorts of problems for the poor conductor.

More successful was a concert on 29 January 1905, organized by the Association of Creative Musicians, which witnessed the premiere of the *Kindertotenlieder* alongside some of the *Wunderhorn* songs. Among those in the audience was Anton von Webern, for whom the piquant, spare orchestration of *Kindertotenlieder* was a revelatory experience and had an unmistakable impact on his own early compositions.

The summer proved to be desperately frustrating for Mahler, who was used to arriving at Maiernigg and letting his inspiration take hold. This time the medicine simply didn't seem to work. Try as he may, the various ideas for the remaining three movements of his *Seventh Symphony* somehow failed to crystallize. Given that it is the most inscrutable of all the symphonies, the one that is by some distance the least popular due to its strangely unsettling atmosphere and lack of any 'big' themes in the manner of his previous works, this is perhaps hardly surprising. He was virtually on the verge of pulling up stumps for the summer when the remainder came to him in a flood of inspiration.

The three central movements of the *Seventh* are the work of a profound genius. Two '*Nachtmusiks*' of a uniquely haunting quality, inhabiting an otherworldliness far removed from convention, frame a scherzo whose sudden 'happenings' are presented in the context of an ethereal, intangible dream world haunted by ghostly imaginings. Here, Mahler's structures are remarkably elastic, as is his use of harmony, whereby chords follow one another with an unconventional fluidity that suavely disarms their underlying revolutionary nature.

The first movement was in fact the last to be composed, and it, too, rejoices in potentially disjointed and tonally unhinging juxtapositions. A slow, typically march-styled introduction leads to an *Allegro* whose changeability is unsettling in its abrupt contrast between militaristic music and a peculiarly hollow-sounding lyricism. The rondo finale has been the subject of more adverse criticism by Mahlerian scholars than any other. Many feel there is an uncharacteristically retrograde look backwards towards the *Wunderhorn* style, others that the obvious cross-referencing to Wagner's *Meistersinger*, not to say the *Adagietto* of his own *Fifth Symphony*, really has no place here. Even the exhilarating finish has been derided as a mechanical-sounding peroration tacked on to the end of the movement, that simply does not sit comfortably with the rest of the work. As with so much music, what on paper may fail to convince can be made to work gloriously in the hands of a first-rate conductor and orchestra.

If Mahler had taken himself near to the brink with his new symphony, so his old colleague and friend Richard Strauss had done so at a similar time in his latest opera, *Salome*. It is hardly a coincidence that the next major works of both composers – Mahler's *Eighth Symphony* and Strauss's opera *Der Rosenkavalier* – reverted to far more comfortable realms of expression. After all, it was Schoenberg himself who spoke of the 'burning' sensation of pushing music to its outer limits at this time. His first purely atonal piece, the 1907 *Second String Quartet*, had almost driven him insane. As a result, Schoenberg regularly withdrew into the well-ordered 'sanity' of tonality throughout his career.

To return to *Salome*, Mahler's fastidiousness and refined taste, coupled with his difficulty in coping with material of an explicitly erotic or sexual nature, made him instinctively opposed to Strauss's musical adaptation of Oscar Wilde's text. Yet viewed objectively he considered it a masterpiece, and certain macabre and claustrophobic aspects of the score found a stablemate in Mahler's own highly complex personality. He therefore planned to stage the premiere in arch-conservative Vienna, but immediately found himself gagged by the censors, who found the various references to Christ untenable. In addition, there was the problem of John the Baptist's appearances on stage, albeit under his Hebrew name, Jochanaan, in the context of a highly sexually-charged production.

Mahler simply wouldn't let go. Letters went back and forth between Mahler, Strauss and the official censor, who was then objecting only to certain textual matters – one can hardly imagine what his reaction would have been if he had witnessed these scenes as enhanced by Strauss's lurid scoring. Mahler, despite instinctively agreeing with much of what the censor said, stuck to his guns, stating on one occasion that 'in art, it is only the *form* that matters, not the *content*.' The arguments roared on throughout the autumn and winter, with the whole thing being used as an excuse for the anti-Mahler brigade to get up on their soapboxes again, citing that in any case he seemed to be spending more time composing and performing his music elsewhere than concentrating his energies on Vienna. From this moment, Mahler's days as director of the Vienna Opera were numbered.

Mahler inadvertently put more fuel on the fire by returning to Amsterdam during the March of 1906, to direct performances of his *Fifth Symphony*, *Kindertotenlieder* and *Das klagende Lied*. He retained a strong affection for this relatively early offering, and once again was full of praise for the technical polish and understanding of the Dutch players and Mengelberg's intuitive understanding of his music. It is an interesting point that in place of Mahler's elemental fire and manic gesturing as a conductor, Mengelberg was all long phrases and nobility – yet both men produced results of extraordinary insight and electricity.

On 16 May, the premiere of Strauss's *Salome* took place belatedly, not in Vienna as everyone had hoped, but in Graz. It caused a sensation, as was almost inevitable, and left Mahler feeling even more despondent about the Viennese and their cliquey conservatism. Artistically, he was at the hub of Europe, yet there was still so much that needed changing. Needless to say, Strauss agreed and advised Mahler to get out of the 'pigsty' as soon as he was able. Mahler was destined to be out of the pigsty quicker than either man could have imagined.

Less than two weeks later, another major premiere took place – the *Sixth Symphony* first saw the light of day on 27 May, as part of the Composers' Festival in Essen, following several days of strenuous rehearsal and furious correcting of orchestral parts. Characteristically it was not so much the emotional impact of the work that Mahler was so concerned about, but the clarity of its orchestration and elucidation of the purely musical argument. This is particularly revealing, coming from a composer for whom the subjective often appears paramount and technique is of only secondary interest. It has been suggested that this may have been due, in part, to his close relationship with Strauss, one of the most intuitive masters of orchestration who ever lived. Mahler never felt entirely satisfied with the scoring of any of his works, whereas Strauss, as he saw it, just seemed to get it right first time, over and over again. For his part, Strauss considered that Mahler's natural insecurity led him to overscore his music. For once the reviews were generous in their praise, several critics referring to the clearer outlines of the symphony and an increased depth of expression imparting a tragic quality to the work.

The summer of 1906 divided roughly into two parts, the first an extraordinary eight-week period at Maiernigg where he composed his vast *Eighth Symphony*, the work he considered his greatest to date. This technicolor blockbuster is a hedonistic amalgam of the medieval Latin hymn, '*Veni, creator spiritus*' ('Come Thou, infinite Creator'), and the closing scene from Part II of Goethe's *Faust*. In recent years it has become customary to feel slightly embarrassed by its sense of overkill – the almost non-stop roller-coaster of thrills and spills of the first movement and the sprawling nature of the hour-long 'finale'. But, bearing in mind that for Mahler the symphony represented an 'entire world', this has to be his archetypal work in that form.

The *Eighth Symphony* is scored for massive forces, including 3 sopranos, 2 contraltos, tenor, baritone, bass, boys' choir, mixed choir, and a huge orchestra featuring 4 flutes, 2 piccolos, 4 oboes, cor anglais, 6 clarinets (2 in E flat), 4 bassoons, contrabassoon, 8 horns, 4 trumpets, 4 trombones, tuba, offstage brass, 2 harps, mandolin, and an array of percussion including celesta, piano, glockenspiel, gong, organ and harmonium. Mahler throws virtually everything at the thrilling first movement, an extraordinary tri-partite setting of '*Veni creator spiritus*' of uncontainable energy and rejoicing. In contrast, the extended finale features sounds of the utmost delicacy and refinement, summoned from the vast instrumental and choral forces at Mahler's disposal. It was to Goethe, the great German poet, that Mahler turned for this gargantuan panoply – the closing scene of *Faust*, in which Faust's soul achieves salvation through the Virgin Mary (Mater Gloriosa). Motifs from the opening movement are subtly fused into this awe-inspiring edifice, a truly life-enhancing fusion of mind and spirit.

The second half of the summer was marked by Mahler's appearances at the Salzburg Mozart Festival, conducting both *The Marriage of Figaro* and *Don Giovanni*. The latter was produced by and starred the legendary Lilli Lehmann, with the usual breath-taking designs by Alfred Roller. *Figaro* featured one of those aberrations that Mahler occasionally indulged in, quite in keeping with the liberties taken by others but arguably a strange lapse of taste for someone of his fabulous abilities and insights. In the second act he interpolated an additional recitative of his own composition in Mozart's style, using some of Beaumarchais's original text. The fact that it appeared as part of what were the one-hundred-and-fiftieth celebrations of Mozart's birth seems quite staggering to our current age of authenticity and period 'correctness'.

The new season was marked by the combined appearance of the great tenor Enrico Caruso and the baritone Titta Ruffo in *Rigoletto* at a gala event on 6 October. Of far greater importance to Mahler, however, was the Viennese premiere of the *Sixth Symphony* on 4 January 1907. The 'antis' were out in force, and since one of their main objections was Mahler's absenteeism, brought about largely by his conducting of his own music, this was doomed from the start. In relation to Mahler's famous blows of fate, one critic noted painfully that: 'Where music falls short, the hammer falls.'

Mahler had no time to count the critical bruises as he shortly departed on yet another break – away from the opera – this time a short tour taking in Berlin, Frankfurt-am-Main and Linz, conducting performances of his *First* and *Third Symphonies*. The Viennese critics saw their chance and during the city's principal conductor's absence, mischievously put it about that Mahler had in fact resigned, and had downed his baton for good to concentrate solely on composition.

Returning to Vienna in the February, Mahler's dismay at Viennese conservatism is illustrated by a concert that featured the premiere of Schoenberg's *Second String Quartet*. This was the work where Schoenberg departed from tonality altogether in the finale, which features a soprano singing the poignant words 'I breathe the strange air from another planet.' Before the work had even got that far, one well-known critic began hissing his contempt. Mahler was on his feet in no time demanding a retraction, and was nearly floored before a friend intervened and cooled the situation down. The following day, Mahler wrote to Strauss recommending the new quartet in the strongest terms, even though in private he confessed to Alma that he had not really understood it.

Mahler's last notable new stage production in Vienna that season was Gluck's *Iphigénie en Aulide* during March 1907, a work that had also attracted Wagner's sincerest attention – the German master had made his own adaptation of Gluck's overture, to which he had added a magical coda.

A disagreement regarding a trip to Rome the same month to direct three more concerts brought the subject of his absenteeism to a head – in fact, to the point of no return. Although the news was somehow kept away from the newspapers to begin with, the critics nevertheless had a field day sneering at his absence in Rome. During May the situation had clearly become so strained that the news of his resignation became official, although no public statement had yet been made. This eventually followed in the June, when Mahler made a formal announcement despite many declarations of devoted support from some of Vienna's most powerful musical figures and intellectuals.

During his tenure at the Vienna Opera, Mahler had presided over a remarkable fifty-two new productions of established repertoire, and introduced no fewer than thirty-two new works to Viennese audiences, many of them of a contemporary nature, such as Puccini's *La Bohème* and *Madama Butterfly*.

Of the various offers that poured in, Heinrich Conried of

New York's Metropolitan Opera House had the upper hand from the outset. He had the 'stars' (many of them from Germany), a superb orchestra and a first-rate set-up. The fees that Mahler was offered were nothing short of astronomical. A contract was signed – he would officially start work at the Met. in January 1908.

Although Mahler was hardly delighted about the move to America, the obvious security as well as the challenge of establishing himself both as a conductor and composer in the New World certainly had their attractions. However, no sooner had he begun to warm to the idea than tragedy struck. In late June, while staying at Maiernigg, Maria his eldest daughter contracted diptheria. For two weeks she bravely struggled on, causing her parents the greatest anxiety. Mahler was deeply affected and spent hours shut away in his bedroom, simply unable to cope with the situation. Alma describes the final night, when a doctor performed a tracheotomy – Mahler was banned to his room and Alma spent the early hours of the morning wandering around the shores of the lake screaming her agonies out loud. The following day, 5 July 1907, Maria breathed her last, the victim of scarlet fever. Alma spent several days in bed in a serious state of shock.

A few days later, Mahler's own health was causing such concern that a doctor was called and after further ministrations from a Viennese expert, hereditary heart disease – obviously from his mother – was diagnosed. Mahler was forbidden to do anything strenuous for the time being. Although no one could be quite certain by how many, Mahler's days were clearly numbered. Given the mood and subject matter of the *Kindertotenlieder*, and the prophecy of his own destruction in the contemporaneous *Sixth Symphony*, Mahler felt that in some way he had foreseen or, even worse, had brought about the recent tragedy and his own incurable condition.

Before taking up his appointment in America, Mahler had some 'spare' time. During October he conducted his final production in Vienna, Beethoven's *Fidelio*, and then visited both Russia and Scandinavia to conduct various works including his *Fifth Symphony*, which received a standing ovation in St Petersburg. Present in the audience that night was the young Igor Stravinsky, himself on the verge of creating a sensation with the first of his Diaghilev ballets, *The Firebird*. It was on this tour that Mahler made his famous encounter with the great Finnish composer, Jean Sibelius, when he declared that 'The symphony must be like the world. It must embrace everything.' This point of view was utterly opposed to Sibelius's own, although the two apparently got on extremely well.

On 24 November, Mahler conducted his farewell concert in Vienna, which featured a breathtaking performance of the *Second Symphony* in the Musikvereinssaal. The little movement in A flat was received with such a storm of applause that it seemed as though Mahler would never be allowed to proceed to the finale. At the end he received an ovation that surpassed any in his long and distinguished career. As a final gesture of appreciation, a large crowd of admirers gathered at the station to see Mahler off, on the morning of 9 December. The New World beckoned.

CHAPTER 7

NEW WORLD FINALE
(1907–11)

- *New York and the Metropolitan Opera*
- *New York Philharmonic Orchestra*
- *Das Lied von der Erde*
- *Ninth and Tenth Symphonies*
- *Marital problems*
- *Freud*
- *Final illness*

everely wounded by the events of the past few months, Mahler arrived in America a rather older but wiser man. He had no intention of conducting beyond his fiftieth year, and simply viewed the American offer as a means of raising sufficient funds for him to retire on and to allow him to survive on his composing to the end of his days. When money began to roll in from the lucrative American contract, he bought some land just south of Vienna in 1910 and arranged for a home to be built there for his semi-retirement the following year – he never got that far.

Although Mahler had decidedly mixed feelings about the new appointment, he could have no complaints about his reception in America, which came as a breath of fresh air after all the squabbles, heckling and political infighting of Vienna. He told inquisitive reporters that he was very much looking forward to his first season, which he hoped would include some orchestral concerts of his own music. His apartment at the Hotel Majestic was palatial compared to anything he had ever experienced before, and even included *two* grand pianos.

Mahler's first Metropolitan production was Wagner's *Tristan und Isolde*, for which he seems to have already adopted a new, relaxed attitude. The orchestra and chorus were immaculately rehearsed, although the 'star' soloists were given a freer reign than they would ever have enjoyed in Vienna. As regards the staging and scenery, Mahler just kept his mouth shut and let them get on with it. The first night was a virtual sell-out and the critics loved it. Richard Aldrich gave a particularly perceptive account in *The New York Times*:

> *It seemed likely last Friday night that he was a man who will give New York music lovers some interesting experiences. His methods in the conductor's chair are straightforward and direct. His beat is uncommonly sharp, decided and angular, and his attention is alertly directed at all points, seemingly at once. It is significant that his left hand was almost constantly used in the* Tristan *performance to check and subdue. He gives the unmistakable impression of a man of commanding authority and of keen insight.*

Mahler's extraordinary impact with this first production was such that, just as he thought he might be able to relax a little more, he was once again drawn into a new political situation. With manager Conried's failing health causing increasing concern, the press enthusiastically threw Mahler's hat into the ring as a contender. In the end, the then head of La Scala, Giulio Gatti-Casazza, got the job, and the up-and-coming Toscanini was invited to take over all Italian productions, with Mahler directing the German repertoire. This did little to ease Mahler's state of mind, which was still less than robust following the death of his daughter. He went through spells lasting several hours when he was utterly inconsolable. In his presence, no one, including himself, ever uttered Maria's name out loud again.

Mahler could hardly prevent himself from trying to produce the best possible standards – a production of *Don Giovanni* already had the critics noting the difference in feel between his treatment and the standard Metropolitan version, which invariably reduced the drama to a series of set pieces for star soloists. However, he had certainly stopped burning the candle at both ends – even Alma referred to him as 'a changed man in New York'. Following the problems and concerns for his health, he seemed far more able to take things as he found them rather than continually aiming for perfection. All the traditional cuts gradually sneaked back into his Wagner productions, and he was, generally speaking, far more gentle with his players and singers.

At the end of the first season, Mahler's contract was renewed for another year, although at his request it gave him more room for manoeuvre to conduct three concerts with the New York Symphony Society. Furthermore, it was arranged that in March and April 1909 he would also conduct a series of four concerts at Carnegie Hall, featuring a hand-picked orchestra of his own choosing.

Mahler spent the summer in Europe, starting with a brief concert tour. He directed the *First Symphony* at Wiesbaden and then two concerts in Prague as part of the Jubilee Exhibition, where the premiere of his *Seventh Symphony* appears to have raised more enthusiasm in terms of the honour so bestowed than anything in particular about the music itself. Otto Klemperer, then conductor of the Prague German Opera Theatre, recalled that Mahler had upwards of two dozen rehearsals with the orchestra, making all the usual corrections and 'improvements' to the scoring as he went along.

During the summer, Mahler discovered a new retreat at Toblach (now Dobbiaco) in Moravia. This would be his last 'composing refuge' – he had sold the house at Maiernigg following the tragedy there the previous year. Mahler's attention now turned to *Die chinesische Flöte* ('The Chinese flute'), a collection of oriental poems in German translations, kindly sent him by a friend. He immediately set about making extensive sketches for a 'symphony' for tenor, contralto (baritone) and orchestra, entitled *Das Lied von der Erde* ('The Song of the Earth'), which was completed the following year. He had no intention of tempting fate by following in the footsteps of Beethoven, Schubert and Bruckner and calling it 'Symphony No.9'. However, he did begin making some purely instrumental sketches, which ultimately evolved into the '*Ninth*' proper. Mahler became increasingly despondent about his heart condition. He could no longer go for the long walks he so loved, and was more or less confined to his composing desk, save for the odd short stroll.

Das Lied von der Erde is a masterly setting of six of the Chinese poems, and many consider it is the finest of all his works. Starting with an earthy drinking song, he takes us on a journey through life's experiences, the final setting representing death not as a violent series of hammer blows in the manner of the *Sixth Symphony*, but as a welcome release, a spiritual transformation as we pass into the next world with the repeated '*Ewig . . . Ewig . . .*' ('Eternally . . . Eternally . . . .').

The opening '*Drinking Song of Earth's Sorrow*' is a strikingly bold creation, a shout of inebriated false confidence in the wake of adversity. The uncompromising ending comes as a stark reminder that Death will not be cheated. An altogether gentler creation is '*The Lonely One in Autumn*', where the sensation of Autumn mists drifting over the lake and predominantly floral imagery unerringly suggested by orchestration is as deft as it is magically half-spoken. The three movements that follow are shorter and generally lighter in tone. 'Youth', a delightful *Allegretto*, tells of young people enjoying a picnic by the waterside, the whole scene being hauntingly inverted by its reflection in a lake. 'Beauty' gently juxtaposes a scene of young maidens collecting flowers with a group of young men trampling by on horseback, while the exuberantly volatile 'Drunkard in Spring' returns us to the swaggering rumbustiousness of the opening song. '*Der Abschied*' ('The Farewell'), a half-hour movement lasting almost as long as the rest of the work put together, is the greatest of all Mahlerian adagios, for many his finest single movement. The orchestration is sparing, lonely woodwind solos are floated over an otherworldly background of ghostly gong resonances and magical timbres. By the end, we arrive transformed, transfigured, as the music simply liquidates. The instruments fall away one by one until we are left as if in suspended animation.

The Mahlers returned to New York by steamer with their remaining three-year-old child, Anna, in November 1908, settling into the Savoy Hotel, which would be Mahler's American base to the end of his days. The season opened with the three New York Symphony Concerts as planned, which included the American premiere of the *Second Symphony*. It would seem that, unaccustomed as the orchestra was to such uncompromising standards – it was not uncommon for members simply not to turn up to rehearsals – on the night they played with a corporate virtuosity that excelled anything New York had heard before. The critics found the symphony's apocalyptic sense of 'overkill' a little *too* much of a good thing, although it was generally recognized as a work of profound feeling and originality. There was also unstinting praise for Mahler's latest production of *The Marriage of Figaro* as the new season got underway, with its added attraction of a harpsichord during the recitatives.

The acclaim in America started to have a positive effect on Mahler, and he began to see life in a more positive light – he lived for every hour. It was also in February 1909 that it had been decided to revive the New York Philharmonic Society on the basis of a regular, full-time professional outfit, that would achieve the highest possible standards in orchestral playing. On 1 April, Mahler conducted their inaugural concert, including a performance of Beethoven's *Symphony No. 7* that had the critics in raptures. He was henceforth signed up as director for the following season and given carte blanche to hire and fire, as well as to try and engage some first-rate European players during the summer break. Needless to say, all this necessitated his resignation from the Met. for the 1909–10 season.

The most important event of the summer was the completion of his *Ninth Symphony* at Toblach, a colossal work in four movements that Mahler mentions in a letter to Bruno Walter would be best placed next to the *Fourth*. The two works are very different in character, the childlike innocence of the earlier work apparently an odd bedfellow for the world-weary acceptance of death of the latter. Perhaps he merely wished to place the best of his last against the best of the past.

The *Ninth* appears, like *Das Lied*, to progress inexorably towards death, yet here there is a disturbing bitterness that its predecessor almost entirely lacks. The musical material constantly varies and develops upon itself, hardly relying at all on normal structural forms or standard repetitions of phrases. This conjures up an almost dream world of musical progression that was to have far-reaching effects upon the expressionist works of Schoenberg, Berg and Webern, both in terms of continual variation structures and subject matter.

The *Ninth Symphony* opens with an *Andante comodo*, which, almost invariably for Mahler, is composed against the background of a march. Music of exquisite resignation is contrasted with full-blown nostalgia, felt not so much as an acute longing as warm reflectiveness. There is very little sense of a death wish here. The cutting edge is unmistakably felt, however, with the bitter irony of the *Ländler* second movement. This casts a painfully cynical eye not only over this traditional peasant dance, but its triple-time ballroom cousin, the waltz, and its classical predecessor, the minuet, en route. The process is taken a stage further with the minor-key Rondo-Burleske marked '*Sehr trotzig*' ('very defiant'), which rants and raves as if locked in the grip of some gruesome obsession. It is only in the finale that some sort of resolution is sought and found – in music of the most profound simplicity and serenity that finds the composer in a mood of calm acceptance with a hint of grim realization. He moves with profound nobility towards his place of eternal rest.

Leaving Alma and Anna in Vienna after returning there in the September (for both required an operation on their tonsils), he made for Göding in Moravia – his real homeland. In a small castle owned by Fritz Redlich, a wealthy industrialist whom the composer had befriended back in 1903, Mahler put the finishing touches to *Das Lied von der Erde*.

Mahler and his family arrived back in New York on 19 October 1909 on the liner, *Kaiser Wilhelm II*, on the same crossing, as it happened, as the world-famous Austrian violinist, Fritz Kreisler. A new chapter of Mahler's life was about to begin with his directorship of the newly-formed Philharmonic. He had been as good as his word and rethought the entire outfit. Only two of the old woodwind players remained, and three of the brass – the rest were all imported continentals. That season Mahler conducted a total of forty-six concerts, including visits with the Philharmonic to several important venues, most memorably Philadelphia and Boston.

A great deal of thought had been put into the programming of these concerts. One special feature was a Beethoven symphony cycle, which included seven of the overtures, but no *First Symphony*! Another was a series of six historical concerts, which were planned to take the listeners through the history of orchestral music from Bach to the present day. It was for the first of these concerts that he made an arrangement of five movements from Bach's *Second* and *Third Orchestral Suites*, including the famous 'Air' from the latter. Mahler apparently directed almost the entire concert from a Steinway grand piano, specially adapted to create a 'twangy' sound roughly reminiscent of a harpsichord but probably sounding more like a fortepiano – not a million miles from

Glenn Gould's famous 'harpsipiano' of the 1950s and '60s.

Mahler's natural enthusiasm had clearly got the better of him, and worries about his health were put on the back-burner. However, it was still his intention to retire from performing in 1911, and concentrate on composing. We learn from a letter to Bruno Walter of December 1909 that his day-to-day existence was now limited to only four activities: 'conducting, transcribing music, eating and sleeping'. His own music had begun to take more of a popular hold via both the *First Symphony* and the *Kindertotenlieder*. The latter's extraordinary intensity of feeling took the New York audience aback at its American premiere.

The new year witnessed one of those historical meetings of musical minds that occurs every so often, bringing together Mahler as conductor and Rachmaninov as pianist, the latter making his first visit to the United States with the freshly-composed *Third Piano Concerto* as his calling card. They gave the third-ever performance on 16 January 1910, which Mahler rehearsed as immaculately as any piece he had ever known. Rachmaninov was greatly impressed by the standard of Mahler's preparations:

> *Mahler then announced that we would play the first movement again. I expected a riot to break out, or at the very least some signs of general unrest from the ranks; but the rehearsal continued as before. Indeed, the orchestra played the first movement with even greater concentration second time around.*

With the orchestral season behind him, on 5 March 1910, Mahler directed the first performance of Tchaikovsky's opera, *The Queen of Spades*, in America – his last-ever production at the Metropolitan, and one that found many of the cast who had known him previously noting how old and tired he now looked. Soloists were lazy about turning up to rehearsals and there were inaccuracies in ensemble and technical infelicities too – these would formerly never have got by him, but he was apparently now resigned to let them through.

Nevertheless, Mahler seems publicly to have been fairly optimistic about his first season at the helm of the Philharmonic at least. Although he cancelled a planned conducting tour in Frankfurt due to sheer exhaustion, an interview in the 30 March edition of the *New York Times* shows him in robust form:

> *I am pleased with the results of my work here. . . . The orchestra had improved from concert to concert, and the attitude of the New York public is always serious and attentive. I have made no plans as yet for my concerts next season . . . I shall divide the programmes more or less evenly between the classic and modern schools. . . .*

Mahler set sail from New York on 5 April, bound for Paris and the French premiere of his *Second Symphony* at the Théâtre du Châtelet eleven days later. From France he travelled to Rome, to give a short series of concerts with the orchestra there, which were of a truly desperate standard. Mahler cancelled the final concert due to 'ill health'. 1910 was Mahler's fiftieth birthday year, however, and rather better things lay just around the corner.

The premiere of the *Eighth Symphony* had been arranged in Munich in celebration of the birthday on 12 September. During May and June, Mahler toured from Vienna to Leipzig to Munich, having preliminary rehearsals with the choruses and the orchestra. The performance was arranged by a concert agency run by the redoubtable Emil Gutmann who – unbeknown to Mahler – was planning to bill the event under the banner '*The Symphony of a Thousand*', a nickname that has stuck to this day.

The premiere of the *Eighth Symphony*, with its breathtaking number of performers assembled in Munich's gargantuan Exhibition Hall was perhaps the greatest single triumph of his entire career. Virtually everyone who had had contact with Mahler over the years was in the audience, and for many (even those who normally fought shy of Mahler's music), this was the most powerful vindication of his genius. Bruno Walter recollected in his 1936 book on the composer:

> *Everyone was utterly in awe of the man, especially the children in the choir, whose hearts he had won from the very first rehearsal. There was this extraordinary moment when with thundering applause all around him, Mahler appeared in front of a thousand performers. . . . As the last notes died away and an incredible ovation burst forth from all around him, he mounted the steps of the auditorium towards where the children's chorus was positioned . . . and shook every one of them personally by the hand.*

Telegrams and well-wishing letters poured in, including one from Schoenberg almost begging him to return to Vienna. The Opera also desperately wanted him back in the light of Weingartner's imminent resignation.

If Mahler's musical life had reached its apotheosis, his personal life was in something of disarray. He had received a letter from an ardent admirer of Alma's, which seemed to imply that she may have been unfaithful. She had not – but confessed to having considered leaving Mahler simply to start a new life on her own. This kindled in him such strong feelings for Alma that he found it impossible to come to terms with the fact that he could have been so emotionally neglectful of her over the years. Indeed, since the death of his daughter, normal sexual relations had effectively ceased. He even managed to convince himself that he might have psychopathic tendencies. So severe was his complex that as a form of emotional release he sketched the first movement of his *Tenth Symphony* – the only one he ever fully completed – in which he poured out his agonies and concerns. This twenty-five-minute movement of the utmost density and harmonic complexity, is punctuated by one chord that contains nearly all of the semitones of the octave simultaneously. It is tantalizing to speculate where such daring might have taken Mahler if he had only been granted more time.

The *Tenth* was originally to have been in five movements (including two scherzos), although only the first movement and twenty-three bars of the third were conclusively orchestrated. As time went by, more and more of Mahler's detailed sketches emerged for the rest of the work and various musicians became involved in trying to produce a performing version – both Schoenberg and Shostakovich turned down invitations to produce a 'definitive' score. Things gathered pace with the work done on the manuscript by the English musicologist Deryck Cooke during the fifties and sixties, who, after several revisions, arrived at his definitive 'performing version' in 1966. The most recently recorded version is by Remo Mazetti Jnr., based not only on Cooke's edition, but two others by Joseph Wheller and an American, Clinton Carpenter. This was published in 1989, the same year as a revision by the British composing brothers, Colin and David Matthews, who had worked with Cooke on his final 1966 revision.

Mahler promptly sought out Sigmund Freud, who was staying in Leiden at the time. Following an informal conversation with Freud one afternoon, everything appears to have become clear to him. Although he had always felt a strong sexual attraction for Alma, his apparent lack of libido was 'diagnosed' as a Holy Mary complex – that a woman of Alma's stature simply shouldn't be defiled by anything as earthly as physical lust. Shortly before the premiere of the *Eighth*, Mahler had written to Alma telling her that he had seen the light and everything would be different from then on. The *Eighth* was dedicated to his beloved Alma.

The new American season got under way on Tuesday 1 November, repeated the following Friday afternoon, thereby establishing a pattern for virtually every week of the forthcoming season. The performance of Schubert's '*Great*' *Symphony in C major* and Strauss's *Also sprach Zarathustra*, which formed part of that historic programme, left the critics gasping for superlatives. Indeed, Mahler was now enjoying the single most extended period of success of his entire career.

A disagreement with the Philharmonic Society over payments for extra concerts seemed to provide the opportunity to bring seriously into question whether he would in fact be returning for the 1911–12 season. Behind his back there were also moves afoot by a vocal minority who wanted far greater control over the music the orchestra played – shades of the hiatus between the London Symphony Orchestra and André Previn in our own time. The situation was brought to a head by a performance of the *Fourth Symphony*, which caused even more problems with complaints of self-interest.

On 21 February 1911, Mahler conducted his last concert with the Philharmonic in Carnegie Hall – it turned out to be his final concert with any orchestra. He was already suffering from a sore throat and high fever and clearly should not have gone through with the engagement, which included the first performance of Busoni's *Berceuse*. Mahler's support for contemporary music had been another of the Philharmonic's frequent quarrels with their Director. Mahler would obviously not be fit enough to conduct again that season. Negotiations with Weingartner were instantly put into place, and there was even a move among the general public to have the orchestra's leader Spiering, installed as conductor after he had 'directed' the orchestra for one concert from the leader's chair. Of concern for Mahler, there was suddenly hardly a sign. Just when Mahler needed their help and support, people began deserting in their droves.

A doctor was called in to try and assess the cause of Mahler's intermittent fevers, and confirmed the suspicion that he was being consumed by a bacterial infection – it was still the era before antibiotics and little could therefore be done. Mahler insisted on knowing the truth and expressed a wish to die in Vienna. This was granted, on condition that he visit a bacteriologist in Paris on the way.

Mahler's light was fading fast. He was barely capable of making the crossing and had to be undressed and dressed and carried onto the sun-deck every day and fed. The Paris bacteriologist could do little but confirm his New York doctor's original diagnosis. His condition was so severe by then that although the French doctors would normally have forbidden the trip to Vienna, it was felt that he had nothing to lose. He travelled by train on a stretcher, arriving in Vienna on 13 May 1911. Five days later he died shortly after 11pm in the Loew Sanatorium, six weeks short of his fifty-first birthday. His last words, as reported by Alma Mahler were: 'Mozart – Mozart!'

His body was buried according to his own wishes in the same grave as his daughter Maria at the cemetery in Grinzing, Vienna. The gravestone is a simple affair designed by Josef Hoffmann, with the great man's name inscribed in capital letters at its head.

◆

Although Mahler was no more, his music lived on. On 20 November 1911, Bruno Walter conducted the world premiere of *Das Lied von der Erde* in Munich, and then the first performance of the *Ninth Symphony* in Vienna the following year. The *Tenth* was first given in Vienna under Franz Schalk in 1924.

Interest in Mahler dwindled during the interwar years, a situation that was hardly helped by the fact that English scholarship became obsessed with the idea of linking Mahler with Bruckner. At least one important and influential volume even placed their life and works side by side. There are certain parallels to be drawn between these two giants of the symphonic arena, although the acid test is the music itself, which is utterly different both in texture and style. A shared propensity for the *Ländler* and a tendency towards composing extended, meditative slow movements sounds more convincing on paper than it ever does in practice.

It is only during the last twenty years or so that Mahler 'fever' can be said to have reached epidemic proportions. Works that were at one time considered 'difficult' both to play and comprehend, have become less daunting. Record companies produce Mahler symphony cycles nowadays with a frequency that might suggest that Beethoven and Brahms are going out of fashion. Indeed the gramophone's power to domesticate even the most profound of musical statements brings the disturbing concept of 'Mahler consumerism' ever closer.

Let us hope, as we enter the new millennium, that Mahler's multifaceted symphonic 'worlds' retain their ability to shock – and to question.

GUSTAV MAHLER: COMPLETE LIST OF WORKS

Herzog Ernst von Schwaben, opera based on Josef Steiner's own libretto, probably from his story *Uhland* (1875, lost)

Violin Sonata (1876, lost)

Piano Quintet (1876, lost)

Piano Quartet in A minor (one movement plus fragment of scherzo, c.1876–78)

Symphony in A minor (three movements in MS, 1876–78)

Scherzo for Piano Quintet (1878, lost)

Die Argonauten, opera on libretto by Mahler, based on Franz Grillparzer (1879–80, lost)

Arrangement of Bruckner's *Third Symphony* for piano duet (?with R. Krzyzanowski, 1880)

Rübezahl, opera based on Mahler's own libretto, in prologue and five acts (c.1879–83, music lost)

(3) *Lieder* (words by Mahler, 1880):
- ◊ '*Im Lenz*' (19 February)
- ◊ '*Winterlied*' (27 February)
- ◊ '*Maitanz im Grünen*' (5 March) – virtually identical to '*Hans und Grethe*' (*see* LIEDER UND GESÄNGE, *overleaf*)

Das klagende Lied (words by Mahler), cantata for soprano,
  contralto, tenor, mixed chorus and orchestra (c.1878–80,
  revised 1892–93 and 1898–99):
  1   '*Waldmärchen*' (Woodland Legend)
  2   '*Der Spielmann*' (The Minstrel)
  3   '*Hochzeitstück*' (Wedding Piece)

Lieder und Gesänge (i), for voice and piano (1880–83):
  1   '*Frühlingsmorgen*' (Leander)
  2   '*Erinnerung*' (Leander)
  3   '*Hans und Grethe*' (Mahler) – virtually identical to
       '*Maitanz im Grünen*' (*see* (3) LIEDER, *above*)
  4   '*Serenade aus Don Juan*' (Tirso de Molina, translated by
       L. Braunfels)
  5   '*Phantasie aus Don Juan*' (Tirso de Molina, translated
       by L. Braunfels)

Lieder eines fahrenden Gesellen (words by Mahler), song cycle
  for low voice and piano/orchestra (c.1883–85, revised
  c.1891–96):
  1   '*Wenn mein Schatz Hochzeit macht*'
  2   '*Ging heut' morgens übers Feld*'
  3   '*Ich hab' ein glühend Messer*'
  4   '*Die zwei blauen Augen*'

Der Trompeter von Säkkingen, incidental music after the play
  by Joseph Victor von Scheffel (1884, lost)

Symphony No.1 in D (c.1884–88, revised 1893–96)

Lieder und Gesänge (ii), for voice and piano from Clemens
  Brentano and Achim von Arnim's *Des knaben Wunderhorn*
  (1887–90):
  1   '*Um schlimme Kinder artig zu machen*'
  2   '*Ich ging mit Lust durch einem grünen Wald*'
  3   '*Aus! Aus!*'
  4   '*Starke Einbildungskraft*'

Lieder und Gesänge (iii), for voice and piano from Brentano and
  Arnim's *Des knaben Wunderhorn* (1887–90):

    1   *'Zu Strassburg auf der Schanz'*
    2   *'Ablösung im Sommer'*
    3   *'Scheiden und Meiden'*
    4   *'Nicht Wiedersehen!'*
    5   *'Selbstgefühl'*

Symphony No.2 in C minor ('*Resurrection*'), for soprano, contralto, mixed choir and orchestra (1884–94, revised 1903)

Reconstruction and completion of Carl Maria von Weber's opera *Die drei Pintos* (1888)

Symphony No.3 in D minor, for contralto, women's choir, boys' choir and orchestra (1893–96, revised 1906)

Des knaben Wunderhorn (Clemens Brentano and Achim von Arnim), songs for voice and piano or orchestra (1892–98):
    1   *'Der Schildewache Nachtlied'* (1892)
    2   *'Verlor'ne Müh'* (1892)
    3   *'Trost im Unglück'* (1892)
    4   *'Wer hat dies Liedlein erdacht?'* (1892)
    5   *'Das irdische Leben'* (1892–93)
    6   *'Des Antonius von Padua Fischpredigt'* (1893)
    7   *'Rheinlegendchen'* (1893)
    8   *'Lied des Verfolgten im Turm'* (1898)
    9   *'Wo die schönen Trompeten blasen'* (1898)
   10   *'Lob des hohen Verstandes'* (1896)
   11   *'Es sungen drei Engel'* (1895)
   12   *'Urlicht'* (c.1892)
        'Das himmlische Leben' (1892)

Symphony No.4 in G, for soprano and orchestra (1892, 1899–1900, revised 1901–10)

7 *Lieder* for voice and orchestra or piano, Nos.1 & 2 from Clemens Brentano and Achim von Arnim's *Des knaben Wunderhorn*; Nos.3–7 are the so-called '*Rückert Lieder*' (1899–1902):
    1   *'Revelge'* (1899)

2 *'Der Tambourg'sell '* (1901)
3 *'Blicke mir nicht in die Lieder'* (1901)
4 *'Ich atmet' einen Linden Duft '* (1901)
5 *'Ich bin der Welt abhanden gekommen'* (1901)
6 *'Um Mitternacht '* (1901)
7 *'Liebst du um Schönheit '* (1902)

Symphony No.5 in C sharp minor (1901–2, scoring revised on
several occasions)

Kindertotenlieder, song cycle for voice and orchestra after
Friedrich Rückert (1901–4):
1 *'Nun will die Sonn' so hell aufgeh'n'*
2 *'Nun seh' ich wohl, warum so dunkle Flammen'*
3 *'Wenn dein Mütterlein'*
4 *'Oft denk' ich, sie sind nur ausgegangen'*
5 *'In diesem Wetter, in diesem Braus'*

Symphony No.6 in A minor (1903–4, revised 1906, scoring revised
on several occasions)

Symphony No.7 in E minor (1904–5, scoring revised on several
occasions)

Symphony No.8 in E flat, for 3 sopranos, 2 contraltos, tenor,
baritone, bass, boys' choir, mixed choir and orchestra
(1906)

Vocal score arrangement of W. A. Mozart's *The Marriage of Figaro*
(1907)

Das Lied von der Erde, symphony for contralto, tenor and
orchestra, from Hans Bethge's *Die chinesische Flöte*
(1908–9)

Symphony No.9 in D (1908–9)

Symphony No.10 in F sharp minor (one movement completed,
1910; Deryck Cooke performing version, 1964, revised
1976)

Suite aus den Orchesterwerken von J.S.Bach for organ, harpsichord and orchestra (1910)

Also vocal score of Weber's *Oberon* (published 1919), and arrangements and performing editions of various works including:
- ◊ Beethoven's *'Choral' Symphony (No.9)* and *F minor String Quartet*, Op. 95
- ◊ Schubert's *'Great' Symphony in C major (No.9)*
- ◊ Schumann's *Symphonies Nos.1–4*
- ◊ Bruckner's *Symphony No.5 in B flat*

GUSTAV MAHLER: RECOMMENDED RECORDINGS

Mahler interpretation is rich and varied enough to fill a book all of its own: from the aerated classicism of George Szell to the almost histrionic passion of Leonard Bernstein; from the more objective stance preferred by Claudio Abbado to the humane warmth of John Barbirolli; from the ennobling utterances of Klaus Tennstedt and Bernard Haitink at their finest to the sheer indomitability of Herbert von Karajan.

All have their admirers and detractors, so that what follows is not so much intended as a list of 'best versions' as a selection of recordings that, between them, represent the astonishingly wide range of approaches on offer.

◆

Suite from Works by Bach; *Symphony No.2 in C minor ('Resurrection') (1st movement only)
◊   Berlin Radio Symphony Orchestra / Peter Ruzicka, *Jésus López-Cobos   ⊗ Koch Schwann 312042

Symphonisches Praeludium (orchestrated by Gürsching); **Symphony No.6 in A minor**
◊   Scottish National Orchestra / Neeme Järvi
     ⊗ Chandos CHAN 9207

Symphonies Nos.1–10 (Adagio)
◊   Various soloists & choirs, Berlin Philharmonic Orchestra, Vienna Philharmonic Orchestra, Chicago Symphony Orchestra / Claudio Abbado   ⊗ DG 447 023-2 (12 discs)

Symphonies Nos.1–9
♦ Various soloists & choirs, Chicago Symphony Orchestra /
Georg Solti ⊗ Decca 430 804-2 (ten discs)

Symphonies Nos.1–4
♦ Edith Mathis (soprano), Doris Soffel (mezzo), Ortrun
Wenkel (contralto), Lucia Popp (soprano), Southend Boys'
Choir, London Philharmonic Orchestra & Choir / Klaus
Tennstedt ⊗ EMI CMS7 64471-2 (4 discs)

Symphony No.1 in D (original 1888 five-movement version, including '*Blumine*')
♦ Scottish National Orchestra / Neeme Järvi
⊗ Chandos CHAN 9308
♦ City of Birmingham Symphony Orchestra / Simon Rattle
⊗ EMI CDC7 54647-2

Symphony No.1 in D (revised 1896–98 version)
♦ Concertgebouw Orchestra / Leonard Bernstein
⊗ DG 427 303-2
♦ London Symphony Orchestra / Georg Solti ⊗ Decca 417 701-2

Symphony No.2 in C minor ('Resurrection')
♦ Sylvia McNair (soprano), Jard van Nes (contralto), Ernst-
Senff Choir, Berlin Philharmonic Orchestra / Bernard
Haitink ⊗ Philips 438 935-2 (2 discs)
♦ Elisabeth Schwarzkopf (soprano), Hilde Rössl-Majdan
(mezzo), Philharmonia Orchestra & Chorus / Otto
Klemperer ⊗ EMI CDM7 69662-2

Symphony No.3 in D minor
♦ Jard van Nes (contralto), Tölz Boys' Choir, Ernst-Senff
Choir, Berlin Philharmonic Orchestra / Bernard Haitink
⊗ Philips 432 162-2 (2 discs)
♦ Janet Baker (mezzo), London Symphony Orchestra &
Chorus / Michael Tilson Thomas ⊗ Sony M2K 44553 (2 discs,
coupled to the 5 *Rückert Lieder*)

Symphony No.4 in G
♦ Judith Raskin (soprano), Cleveland Orchestra / George

Szell ⊗ Sony SBK 46535 (coupled to *Lieder eines fahrenden Gesellen* – von Stade / LPO / A. Davis)

◊ Edith Mathis (soprano), Berlin Philharmonic Orchestra / Herbert von Karajan ⊗ DG 419 863-2

Symphonies Nos.5, 9 & 10 (Adagio)

◊ London Philharmonic Orchestra / Klaus Tennstedt
⊗ EMI CMS7 64481-2 (3 discs)

Symphony No.5 in C sharp minor

◊ New Philharmonia Orchestra / John Barbirolli
⊗ EMI CDM7 64749-2

◊ Vienna Philharmonic Orchestra / Leonard Bernstein
⊗ DG 423 608-2

Symphonies Nos.6, 7 & 8

◊ Elisabeth Connell (soprano), Edith Wiens (soprano), Felicity Lott (soprano), Trudeliese Schmidt (mezzo), Nadine Denize (mezzo), Richard Versalle (tenor), Jorma Hynninen (baritone), Hans Sotin (bass), Tiffin School Boys' Choir, London Philharmonic Orchestra & Choir / Klaus Tennstedt ⊗ EMI CMS7 64476-2 (4 discs)

Symphony No.6 in A minor

◊ *Christa Ludwig (mezzo), Berlin Philharmonic Orchestra / Herbert von Karajan ⊗ DG 415 099-2 (2 discs, coupled to the *5 *Rückert Lieder*)

◊ Concertgebouw Orchestra / Riccardo Chailly ⊗ Decca 444 871-2 (2 discs, coupled to Zemlinsky: *Maeterlinck Lieder*)

Symphony No.7 in E minor

◊ Berlin Philharmonic Orchestra / Bernard Haitink ⊗ Philips 434 997-2 (2 discs, coupled to the *Adagio* from the *10th Symphony*)

◊ City of Birmingham Symphony Orchestra / Simon Rattle
⊗ EMI CDC7 54344-2

Symphony No.8 in E flat ('Symphony of a Thousand')

◊ Cheryl Studer (soprano), Angela Maria Blasi (soprano), Sumi Jo (soprano), Waltraud Meier (mezzo), Kazuko Nagai (mezzo), Keith Lewis (tenor), Thomas Allen (baritone),

Hans Sotin (bass), Southend Boys' Choir, Philharmonia
Orchestra & Chorus / Giuseppi Sinopoli ⊗ DG 435 433-2

◊ Heather Harper (soprano), Lucia Popp (soprano), Arleen
Augér (soprano), Yvonne Minton (mezzo), Helen Watts
(contralto), René Kollo (tenor), John Shirley-Quirk
(baritone), Martti Talvela (bass), Vienna Boys' Choir,
Vienna State Opera Chorus, Vienna Singverein, Chicago
Symphony Orchestra / Georg Solti ⊗ Decca 448 293-2

Symphony No.9 in D

◊ Berlin Philharmonic Orchestra / John Barbirolli
⊗ EMI CDM7 63115-2

◊ *Christa Ludwig (mezzo), Berlin Philharmonic Orchestra /
Herbert von Karajan ⊗ DG 439 678-2 (2 discs, coupled to
*Kindertotenlieder; 5 Rückert Lieder)

Symphony No.10 in F sharp minor

◊ Bournemouth Symphony Orchestra / Simon Rattle
⊗ EMI CDC7 54406-2

◊ Berlin Radio Symphony Orchestra / Riccardo Chailly
⊗ Decca 444 872-2 (2 discs, coupled to Schoenberg: Verklärte Nacht)

Piano Quartet Movement in A minor

◊ Domus ⊗ Virgin VC7 59144-2 (coupled with Brahms: Piano Quartet
No.2)

Kindertotenlieder; Lieder eines fahrenden Gesellen; 5 Rückert Lieder

◊ Janet Baker (mezzo), New Philharmonia Orchestra, Hallé
Orchestra / John Barbirolli ⊗ EMI CDC7 47793-2

Kindertotenlieder; Lieder eines fahrenden Gesellen; 4 Rückert Lieder

◊ Dietrich Fischer-Dieskau (baritone), Berlin Philharmonic
Orchestra, Karl Böhm; Bavarian Radio Symphony
Orchestra / Rafael Kubelik ⊗ DG 415 191-2

Das Klagende Lied

◊ Susan Dunn (soprano), Markus Baur (treble),
Brigitte Fassbaender (mezzo), Werner Hollweg (tenor),

Andreas Schmidt (baritone), Düsseldorf State
Musikverein, Berlin Radio Symphony Orchestra / Riccardo
Chailly   ⊗ Decca 425 719-2

Lieder aus 'Des knaben Wunderhorn'

◊   Elisabeth Schwarzkopf (soprano), Dietrich Fischer-
   Dieskau (baritone), London Symphony Orchestra /
   George Szell   ⊗ EMI CDC7 47277-2
◊   Thomas Hampson (baritone), Geoffrey Parsons (piano)
   ⊗ Teldec 9031 74726-2

Lieder aus 'Des knaben Wunderhorn';
Lieder eines fahrenden Gesellen;
11 Lieder und Gesänge; 4 Rückert Lieder

◊   Christa Ludwig (mezzo), Dietrich Fischer-Dieskau
   (baritone), Walter Berry (bass), Leonard Bernstein
   (piano)   ⊗ Sony SM2K 47170 (2 discs)

Das Lied von der Erde

◊   Janet Baker (mezzo), James King (tenor), Concertgebouw
   Orchestra / Bernard Haitink   ⊗ Philips 432 279-2
◊   Christa Ludwig (mezzo), René Kollo (tenor), Berlin
   Philharmonic Orchestra / Herbert von Karajan
   ⊗ DG 419 058-2

Lieder und Gesänge (some orchestrated by Berio);
Im Lenz; Winterlied; Meltanz im Grünen;
Lieder eines fahrenden Gesellen

◊   Thomas Hampson (baritone), David Lutz (piano),
   Philharmonia Orchestra / Luciano Berio
   ⊗ Teldec 9031 74002-2

Lieder und Gesänge; Lieder eines fahrenden Gesellen;
Im Lenz; Winterlied

◊   Janet Baker (mezzo), Geoffrey Parsons (piano)
   ⊗ Hyperion CDA 66100

SELECTED FURTHER READING

Research on Mahler has come on in leaps and bounds in recent years, spearheaded in Great Britain by the pioneering Donald Mitchell. His three volumes are required reading for all serious Mahler scholars, but any of the following will repay investigation.

Kurt Blaukopf: *Mahler: A Documentary Study* (Thames and Hudson, 1976)

James Burnett: *The Music of Gustav Mahler* (Fairleigh Dickinson University Press, 1986)

Deryck Cooke: *Gustav Mahler: An Introduction to His Music* (Faber, 1980, revised 1988)

Henry-Louis de la Grange: *Vienna: The Years of Challenge, 1897–1904* (Oxford University Press, 1995)

Michael Kennedy: *Mahler* (Dent / Oxford University Press, 1974, revised 1990)

Donald Mitchell: *Gustav Mahler: The Early Years* (Faber, 1958, revised 1980, 1995)

Donald Mitchell: *Gustav Mahler: The Wunderhorn Years* (Faber, 1975, revised 1995)

Donald Mitchell: *Gustav Mahler: Songs and Symphonies of Life and Death* (Faber, 1985)

Zoltan Roman: *Gustav Mahler's American Years, 1907–11* (Pendragon, 1989)

Index

Mahler, Justine, 10, 38, 39, 47, 52, 56, 61
Mahler, Leopoldine, 8, 38
Mahler, Maria Anna ('Putzi'), 62, 66, 74, 77, 84
Mahler, Marie, 8, 38
Mahler, Otto, 10, 38, 47
Manheit, Jacques, 26
Marschalk, Max, 33
Mascagni, Pietro
L'Amico Fritz, 43
Matthews, Colin & David, 84
Mazetti Jnr., Remo, 84
Méhul, Nicholas Etienne
Joseph, 27
Mendelssohn, Felix
Capriccio brillant, 24
St Paul, 29
Mengelberg, Willem, 65, 70
Meyerbeer, Giacomo, 32
Les Huguenots, 26
Mitchell, Donald, 101
Mozart, W.A., 7, 10, 27, 52, 54
Don Giovanni, 10, 27, 30, 40, 72, 77
The Magic Flute, 24, 43, 52
The Marriage of Figaro, 52, 72, 79
Symphony No.40 in G minor, 31, 61

N
Neumann, Angelo, 30
Nietsche, Friedrich Wilhelm
Also sprach Zarathustra (philosophical work), 49, 85
Nikisch, Artur, 30, 31, 32, 48

O
Offenbach, Jacques
The Tales of Hofmann, 60

P
Paul, Jean
Titan (novel), 43
Pollini, Bernhard, 40, 43, 49
Previn, André, 85

Puccini, Giacomo
La Bohème, 73
Madama Butterfly, 73
Manon Lescaut, 42

R
Rachmaninov, Sergei, 82
Piano Concerto No.3, 82
Redlich, Fritz, 81
Richter, Hans, 42, 53, 54, 56
Richter, Johanna, 28, 29
Roller, Alfred, 63, 68, 72
Rosé, Arnold, 10, 52, 61
See also Rosenbaum, Arnold
Rosé, Eduard, 10, 52
Rosenbaum, Arnold, 16
See also Rosé, Arnold
Rossini, Gioachino
The Barber of Seville, 24
Rott, Hans, 15–16, 23
Rubinstein, Anton
The Demon, 53
Rückert, Friedrich, 66
Ruffo, Titta, 72

S
Saint-Saëns, Camille
Danse Macabre, 57
Schalk, Franz, 33, 86
Scharwenka, Xaver
Piano Concerto No.1, 18
Scheu, Josef, 58
Schiedermair, Ludwig, 57
Schindler, Alma, 59, 60, 61
See also Mahler, Alma
Schindler, Anton, 59
Schoenberg, Arnold, 7, 65, 69, 80, 84
String Quartet No.2, 69, 73
Schott (music publishers), 45
Schubert, Franz, 78
Piano Sonata No.16 in A minor, 16–17
Symphony No.9 in C major 'Great', 85
'Wanderer' Fantasy, 18
Schumann, Robert, 24
Humoreske, 17

Shostakovich, Dmitri, 7, 84
Sibelius, Jean, 7, 75
Sittard, Joseph, 41
Slezak, Leo, 58
Steiner, Joseph, 13
Stockhausen, Karlheinz, 7
Strauss, Richard, 32, 46, 47, 55,
  60, 61, 70, 71, 73
  Aus Italien, 54
  Feuersnot, 61
  Guntrum, 46
  Der Rosenkavalier, 69
  Salome, 69–70
Stravinsky, Igor
  The Firebird, 74
Suppé, Franz von
  Boccaccio, 25
Szell, George, 95

T

Tchaikovsky, Piotr, 14, 34, 42
  Eugene Onegin, 42
  The Queen of Spades, 82
Tennstedt, Klaus, 95
Thalberg, Sigismond
  *Fantasia on Themes from Bellini's
  'Norma'*, 12
Toscanini, Arturo, 77
Treiber, Wilhelm, 28, 29

U

Uberhorst, Karl, 27

V

Verdi, Giuseppe
  Aida, 59
  Falstaff, 42
  Rigoletto, 72
  Il Trovatore, 23
Vienna Conservatory, 13

von Scheffel, Victor
  Der Trompeter von Säkkingen
  (poem), 29
Von Mildenburg, Anna, 48, 52

W

Wagner, Richard, 16, 20, 27, 52,
  53–54, 78
  Götterdämmerung, 19, 38
  Lohengrin, 27, 40, 43, 51–52
  Die Meistersinger, 30, 49, 69
  Parsifal, 30
  Das Rheingold, 30, 31, 37
  Ring cycle, 30, 31, 37, 53
  Siegfried, 38, 41, 43, 52
  Tannhäuser, 16, 41
  Tristan und Isolde, 41, 43, 49,
  63, 76, 77
  Die Walküre, 30, 31, 37, 43, 52
Walter, Bruno, 46, 58, 59, 65, 68,
  80, 82, 82, 86
Weber, Carl, 32
Weber, Carl Maria von
  Die drei Pintos, 32, 34
  Der Freischütz, 20, 24, 28
Weber, Marion, 33
Webern, Anton von, 7, 66, 68,
  80
Weingartner, Felix, 47, 84, 85
Wheller, Joseph, 84
Wilde, Oscar, 70
Wolf, Hugo, 15–16, 19, 53, 55,
  57, 63–64
  Der Corregidor, 53

Z

Zemlinsky, Alexander von, 59,
  60, 65
Zichy, Count Géza, 40
Zuckerkandl, Berta, 59

THE
CLASSIC *f*M
GUIDE TO
CLASSICAL MUSIC

JEREMY NICHOLAS

'... a fascinating and accessible guide ... it will provide
an informative and illuminating source of insight
for everybody from the beginner to the musicologist.'

Sir Edward Heath

The Classic fM Guide to Classical Music opens with a masterly
history of classical music, illustrated with charts and lifelines, and
is followed by a comprehensive guide to more than 500 composers. There are major entries detailing the lives and works of the
world's most celebrated composers, as well as concise biographies
of more than 300 others.

This invaluable companion to classical music combines extensive
factual detail with fascinating anecdotes, and an insight into the
historical and musical influences of the great composers. It also
contains reviews and recommendations of the best works, and
extensive cross-references to lesser-known composers. Jeremy
Nicholas's vibrant, informative and carefully researched text is
complemented by photographs and cartoons, and is designed for
easy reference, with a comprehensive index.

£19.99 ISBN: 1 85793 760 0 Hardback
£9.99 ISBN: 1 86205 051 1 Paperback

CLASSIC *f*M
COMPACT COMPANIONS

CHOPIN, PUCCINI, ROSSINI, TCHAIKOVSKY

In association with *Classic fM* and *Philips Classics*, this revolutionary new series, **Compact Companions**, is a stylish package of book and compact disc. Each title provides the ultimate prelude to the lives and works of the most popular composers of classical music.

These composers' extraordinary, eventful lives and their powerful, moving music make them the ideal subjects for combined reading and listening. Written by respected authors, the texts provide a comprehensive introduction to the life and work of the composer, and each includes a richly illustrated biography, a complete list of works and a definitive list of recommended recordings. The accompanying CD combines both favourite and less-well-known pieces, recorded by artists of world renown.

Chopin
Christopher Headington
ISBN: 1 85793 655 8

Puccini
Jonathon Brown
ISBN: 1 85793 660 4

Rossini
David Mountfield
ISBN: 1 85793 665 5

Tchaikovsky
David Nice
ISBN: 1 85793 670 1

£9.99 (inc. VAT) each companion

These books can be ordered direct from the publisher.
Please contact the Marketing Department.
But try your bookshop first.

CLASSIC *f*M
LIFELINES

With 4.8 million listeners every week, *Classic fM* is now the most listened-to national commercial radio station in the UK. With the launch of *Classic fM Lifelines*, Pavilion Books and *Classic fM* are creating an affordable series of elegantly designed short biographies that will put everyone's favourite composers into focus.

Written with enthusiasm and in a highly accessible style, the *Classic fM Lifelines* series will become the Everyman of musical biographies. Titles for the series have been chosen from *Classic fM*'s own listener surveys of the most popular composers.

TITLES PUBLISHED:

Johannes Brahms
Jonathon Brown
ISBN: 1 85793 967 0

Claude Debussy
Jonathon Brown
ISBN: 1 85793 972 7

Edward Elgar
David Nice
ISBN: 1 85793 977 8

Gustav Mahler
Julian Haylock
ISBN: 1 85793 982 4

Sergei Rachmaninov
Julian Haylock
ISBN: 1 85793 944 1

Franz Schubert
Stephen Jackson
ISBN: 1 85793 987 5

£4.99 each book

FORTHCOMING TITLES:

- *J.S. Bach*
- *Ludwig van Beethoven*
- *Benjamin Britten*

- *Joseph Haydn*
- *Dmitri Shostakovich*
- *Ralph Vaughan Williams*

CLASSIC *f*M
LIFELINES

To purchase any of the books in the *Classic fM Lifelines* series
simply fill in the order form below and post or fax it,
together with your remittance, to the address below.

Please send the titles ticked below
(*published spring 1997)

Johannes Brahms	☐	*J.S. Bach	☐
Claude Debussy	☐	*Ludwig van Beethoven	☐
Edward Elgar	☐	*Benjamin Britten	☐
Gustav Mahler	☐	*Joseph Haydn	☐
Sergei Rachmaninov	☐	*Dmitri Shostakovich	☐
Franz Schubert	☐	*Ralph Vaughan Williams	☐

Number of titles @ £4.99 _____   Value: £_____

Add 10% of total value for postage and packing   Value: £_____

Total value of order: £_____

I enclose a cheque (UK only) payable to Pavilion Books Ltd ☐

OR

Please charge my credit card account ☐

I wish to pay by: Visa ☐ MasterCard ☐ Access ☐ American Express ☐

Card number ☐☐☐☐☐☐☐☐☐☐☐☐☐☐☐☐☐☐☐

Signature_____   Expiry Date_____

Name _____

Address _____

_____

_____   Postcode_____

Please send your order to: Marketing Department, Pavilion Books Ltd,
26 Upper Ground, London SE1 9PD, or fax for quick dispatch to:
Marketing Department, 0171-620 0042.